I0569788

The Gospel of God

PLAIN AND SIMPLE

Charles Cooper

Thorns and Gold Publishing
Winter Garden, FL

Thorns and Gold Publishing
P.O. Box 3285
Windermere, FL 34786

Printed in the United States of America

Ordering Information:
Quantity sales. Special discounts are available on quantity purchases by corporations, associations, and others. Contact the "Special Sales Department" at the address above for details.

The Gospel of God: Plain and Simple. —1st ed.
ISBN 979-8-9886537-2-1

All text italicized within Scripture quotes is the author's emphasis, not the original translation.

Contents

Dedication to
Carrli Cooper

The Short of It

The proverbial saying is true in this case. Assuming that the Gospel of God and the Gospel of Christ refer to the same thing is literally trying to squeeze a round peg in a square hole.

Essentially, Jesus preached two significant sermons during his earthly ministry. Both can correctly be identified as gospels. The first sermon focused on the good news from God and concerned the kingdom of God. The second sermon focused on the death, burial, and resurrection of Jesus Christ for the forgiveness of mankind's sins. Over 1500 years, these messages slowly joined, with the Gospel of God losing all distinctions. The good news about Jesus Christ became the single focus of most Christians.

This book is a serious effort to clarify this problem and to reclaim the rightful proclamation of God's intent to set his Son, Jesus, upon the earth as the sovereign ruler with men and women as his assistants.

This is the Gospel of God, plain and simple.

Preface

The Bible is a story that develops over time, just like any other story. If one does not understand this reality, one risks misunderstanding specific Scripture passages. This is especially true in the Matthew, Mark, Luke, and John.

Consider the storyline of your favorite book or movie. As the plot unfolds, more information about the main characters is revealed, especially near the end. For this reason, the car ride home from seeing a good movie is full of conversation about all the connections from the movie's beginning that do not make sense until the end. These connections are what make for an enjoyable film, but one must remember their unique perspective from the seat of the movie theater. As a viewer, you have information that some main characters do not. As the movie pans to the villain's secret lair, the main character does not know its location until later. In the same way, this principle especially applies when you read the books of Matthew, Mark, and Luke. The disciples of Jesus were still physically with him for most of these accounts, as he had not yet been put to death by the Roman Empire and raised three days later.

The dominant message of Jesus' teaching before he arose on that third day was the "gospel" about the kingdom of God (GKG). After the resurrection, the primary emphasis became the "gospel" about Jesus Christ (GJC). As we will show, these two "gospels" are not interchangeable. Seeing these two uses of the word "gospel" as the same will lead to confusion and errors in how we interpret Scripture. So, there is much urgency in understanding this issue.

Failure to recognize the difference between Jesus's pre-resurrection message and the church's post-resurrection message can have profound consequences for correctly interpreting passages in the N.T., particularly the Gospels of Matthew, Mark, and Luke. This underscores the importance of your role in correct interpretation and how integral you are to the process.

Bible translations contribute to this problem. Because few believers know biblical languages, they must trust a translation without understanding the significant decisions about how words and ideas were translated from the original Hebrew or Greek into the modern language. Take the noun *euaggelion*, typically translated as "gospel." Because the church now uses the term "gospel" to refer to the death, burial, and resurrection of Jesus Christ (the Gospel, capital G), it is assumed that any occurrence of this term in our English translations of the NT is shorthand for this. This assumption can lead to a serious misreading of the Gospels, highlighting the gravity of the issue.

A rule of practice for studying the Bible correctly requires every word to be defined according to its context. If, for example, I say the word "king" in a sentence, you would picture a person if we were speaking about England. However, "king" means something entirely different if we play chess together. In the same way that the King of England is not to be confused with a four-inch-tall piece of plastic, the context of a sentence is truly "king."

CHAPTER ONE

The Forgotten "Gospel": The Good News Jesus Preached

Defining "the Gospel"

How many languages do you know? Or how many do some of your friends or family know? Defining the word "gospel" in the New Testament helps us step back and understand that language is an incredible phenomenon. Children grow up not only learning their native language but also the thousands of nuances within that language. This is why translation is so complicated and why your friends who know multiple languages take longer than expected when you ask them what they just said:

"Hey, what did you just say to that person?"
"Well ... basically, I said this."
"What do you mean, basically?"
"That's what it means, but I do not know how to translate it literally."

For this reason, it has been said that "translation is treason" since much of a language's significance is lost in translation.

Not only is this true between two modern languages, but consider how language changes over thousands of years. Modern Greek, for example, differs from Ancient Greek, which Jesus would have heard 2000 years ago, though the alphabet may still be nearly identical.

What do you think of when you hear the word "gospel?" For example, Mark 1:1 opens with, "The beginning of the gospel of Jesus Christ, the Son of God." One must ask, "What meaning does Mark intend by the phrase 'the gospel of Jesus

1

Christ'?" In modern English, the term "gospel" has come to refer to one of three things: the death, burial, and resurrection of Jesus (DBRJC) for the atonement for sin (or the Gospel, capital "G"); the first four books of the New Testament—the gospels of Matthew, Mark, Luke, and John; and lastly, to tell the truth ("You can take that as gospel").

More than likely, if someone says the word "gospel," you think of the first example, where the gospel refers to the story of who Jesus is and what he did by dying on the cross and rising again to atone for sin. But at what point during the development of the New Testament did the definition of the term "gospel" narrow to refer to Jesus' atoning sacrifice only? When did the Greek noun become the exclusive shortened way of referring to the DBRJC for the atonement of man's sin? In other words, if "gospel" can only refer to DBRJC, how can Jesus use it this way before he dies and rises again? Serious error results when one assumes that at the beginning of Jesus' public ministry, everyone using the term "gospel" (John the Baptist, then Jesus, and the subsequent apostles) did so with this singular meaning.

A Historical Perspective

One of the best ways to start is by looking backward to understand what words mean. For example, studying the Greek New Testament helps to begin by looking at the Old Testament. However, one quickly discovers that the Greek noun for "gospel" does not appear in the Greek translation of the Old Testament at all, although another form of the noun occurs several times. The Greek noun is not found in any writings before the letters of the New Testament. Scholars debate whether Paul wrote 1 Thessalonians or Galatians first as the very first book of the New Testament. However, both have the Greek noun in them. The noun only occurs in the gospels of Matthew and Mark, which many agree were written possibly after the letters of Paul.

While we would be right in examining the use of the noun in these two Gospels, it is also helpful to explore Luke and John, which do not use it. This alone should cause all to proceed with caution. If the most "gospel" of the Gospels—John, which focuses on salvation more than any other, does not utilize it to describe the message of Jesus Christ, the obvious question is why? This strongly suggests that the use of this term, in the technical sense, to refer to Jesus' death, burial, and resurrection as the atonement for mankind's sin was not yet in use. Indeed, the church did not use the term this way until after Pentecost. Between the ascension of the Lord Jesus and the first written book of the New Testament is probably twenty-plus years. This special usage would have developed during this period.

If this use of the term did not start until after Pentecost, it casts tremendous doubt that it was used this way during Jesus' earthly ministry. To his audience, our Lord was still Jesus of Nazareth, introducing the good news from God about the coming kingdom. Understanding the term's historical development is critical to correctly interpreting the Gospels.

To pause for a moment, it may be helpful to think of a modern example of a word developing over time. Our discussion here of the word "gospel" is happening 2,000 years after its development, so perhaps it is difficult to wrap our minds around this.

Of all the words you say during the day, let's take one of your top ten vocabulary words: "Google." There may even be parents celebrating right now over their child's first word—"Google." We "Google" everything almost daily and have a wealth of information at our fingertips using our phones.

However, Google is approaching its 26th birthday at the time of this writing. Many readers remember a time without Google or the Internet, but now life seems impossible without it.

Even so, Google has become so integrated into our lives that we do not search for things on the Internet without using Google; Google itself has become a verb. In everyday vocabulary, to "Google" something means to search for information online, whether one uses Google, Bing, or any other search engine.

So, we take this example back to our discussion of the word "gospel." Think about the potential for the word "gospel" to develop significantly over time, as the disciples of Jesus believed that the ultimate "good news" was Jesus' life, death, burial, and resurrection for the forgiveness of sins. But this reality was only understood after the resurrection. Jesus's disciples did not know that he had to die on the cross.

The first time Jesus told his disciples about his coming death, Peter rebuked him (Matt. 16:21–23). Given Peter's response, there is no way Peter understood the need for Jesus to die. When one understands that this incident occurred a little over six months before our Lord's death, it requires the reader to be cautious. How could Peter understand the term "gospel" to refer to Jesus' death, burial, and resurrection when he did not believe that Jesus would have to die at all at this late period in Jesus' ministry?

Even after Jesus' resurrection, the truth of the modern Gospel was still *unknown* to the Twelve. On the third day after our Lord's death, Luke 24:13–21 reports,

> That very day two of them were going to a village named Emmaus, about seven miles from Jerusalem, and they were talking with each other about all these things that had happened. While they were talking and discussing

together, Jesus himself drew near and went with them. But their eyes were kept from recognizing him. And he said to them, "What is this conversation that you are holding with each other as you walk?" And they stood still, looking sad. Then one of them, named Cleopas, answered him, "Are you the only visitor to Jerusalem who does not know the things that have happened there in these days?" And he said to them, "What things?" And they said to him, "Concerning Jesus of Nazareth, a man who was a prophet mighty in deed and word before God and all the people, and how our chief priests and rulers delivered him up to be condemned to death and crucified him. *But we had hoped that he was the one to redeem Israel.* Yes, and besides all this, it is now the third day since these things happened. (emphasis added)

Cleopas makes clear that with the death of Jesus of Nazareth, the apostles' hopes of Israel's redemption were dashed (v. 17). In the eyes of the two on the road to Emmaus, the death of Jesus had no benefit for National Israel. The idea that they understood Jesus' death as having a spiritual benefit for all mankind requires reading later knowledge back into the text.

The "Gospel" in the Parable of the Sower

Many scholars make this same error in the parable of the sower.[1] In his book, John MacArthur transfers the meaning of "the Gospel" to the phrase "the Word of God." He writes,

> *Now alone with the disciples and other inquisitive believers (Mark 4:10), the Lord took what seemed like a simple, obvious story and used it to unveil the magnificent reality of the kingdom.*
>
> *The seed he spoke of was not [a] literal seed, but rather the gospel: "When anyone hears the word of the kingdom . . ." (v. 19). The seed is the message about the King and his kingdom. Luke 8:11, a parallel account, is even more explicit: "The seed is the Word of God." Thus the sower is anyone who plants the seed of the gospel by the Word of God (cf. 1 Peter 1:23) in the heart of an individual. The prototype of all sowers is the Lord himself. (emphasis added)[2]*

This transfer of meaning might go unnoticed by the uninformed reader. However, for one who is careful, it should not. Is MacArthur justified in reading the modern Gospel into this parable as equivalent to the Word of God, i.e., the DBRJC?

As considered above, context is always "king." The circles of context are words, phrases, sentences, paragraphs, chapters, individual books, sections of books, and the complete Old and New Testaments. One first discovers the possible meanings of particular words from the lexicon. Second, one looks at how the author uses the word throughout his writings. Next, one looks at how other writers used the term. Lastly, if possible, one may look at how the term was used outside the Bible in secular writings. The circles of context are an interpreter's best friend.

"Son of Man Is Lifted Up"

We see confirmation of this conclusion in John 12:1. Here, the text informs the reader that "[s]ix days before the Passover, Jesus, therefore, came to Bethany, where Lazarus was, whom Jesus had raised from the dead." In less than a whole week, our Lord would be put to death on the evening before Passover begins. Thus, chapters 12–19 of John's Gospel focus on the Lord's final week before his death on the cross. So, less than six days before the Lord Jesus died, the crowds heard him say,

> "Now is the judgment of this world; now will the ruler [Satan] of this world be cast out. And I, when I am lifted up from the earth, will draw all people to myself." (John 12:31–32)

The reader must understand that when Jesus said this, it was less than six full days before his death. The apostle John adds this comment in the text: "He said this to show by what kind of death he was going to die." This editorial comment of John is his reflection on our Lord's comment thirty-plus years later. When Jesus first said these words, we are convinced that John did not know this fact then. John says the Jewish crowd listening to the Lord's statement understood what he meant by saying, "And I, when I am lifted up from the earth."

We cannot emphasize enough that this is the first time Jesus said he is going to die to a group larger than his original Twelve. John writes,

> So the crowd answered him, "We have heard from the Law that Christ remains forever. How can you say that the Son of Man must be lifted up? Who is this Son of Man?"

The response of the crowd is hugely insightful. First, they understood the phrase "the Son of Man must be lifted up" to mean death. Thus, if Jesus is "the Son of Man," which he claims, and if "the Son of Man" is another way of referring to the Messiah, which the Jews seem to have accepted, then Jesus' statement that "the Son of Man must be lifted up" is a contradiction of their understanding of the Old

Testament Scriptures. At the time, the commonly accepted doctrine among the Jews was that the Messiah would come as a political and military leader who would free the Jews from the oppression of Rome. This expectation did not include the death of the Messiah. Scholars recognize that the idea of the Messiah dying was not a part of the standard theological teachings of the Jewish faith.

Regarding the Jewish response in John 12:34, George R. Beasley-Murray, in the *Word Biblical Commentary,* adds,

> *The crowd voices a difficulty which the representatives of Jesus were to face from Good Friday onward. The "Law" (= the OT, supremely represented by the Law) says that the Messiah remains "forever"...*
>
> *For most Jews the perpetuity of the kingdom of God included the continuance of the Messiah. . . The crowd therefore asks, "How can the Son of Man-Messiah be 'lifted up,' and so removed from the earthly scene by death?" Their further query, "Who is this Son of Man?" means, "What sort of a Son of Man is this, of whom such an unheard-of fate is spoken?"[3]*

The apparent contradiction between what the crowd believed about the Messiah and what Jesus taught about himself is evident. In other words, if Jesus taught from day one that he was going to die, there would not have been any confusion voiced by the people. Up to the very day of Jesus' death, the people did not believe the Messiah must die for their sins to be forgiven. The general idea about the Messiah, according to the Jewish people, nowhere included his death to bring freedom to the Nation. As we shall see, neither did the Twelve, who had objected strenuously to our Lord's prediction of his death about six months earlier.

Thus, the term "gospel," even if it shifted in meaning over time, can only be interpreted correctly in Matthew and Mark's Gospels with a proper context. Considering that context, it becomes clear how easily words can be falsely interpreted, including the Greek term "the gospel." Therefore, before Jesus ascends to heaven, we must continue our work to understand what Jesus meant by "the gospel" before his death, burial, and resurrection.

CHAPTER TWO

The Good News About Jesus Christ

The first question we must answer concerns how the distinction between the gospel of God and the gospel about Christ was lost. It primarily began with the languages of the N.T.

The Gospel of John reports, that Pilate, who put the Lord Jesus to death, had an inscription placed above his head on the cross, "Jesus of Nazareth, the King of the Jews." Concerning this inscription, John 19:20 reports:

> Many of the Jews read this inscription, for the place where Jesus was crucified was near the city, and it was written in Aramaic, in Latin, and in Greek.

Aramaic was the Hebrew people's language, Latin was Rome's official language, and Greek was the world's common language. The role these three languages will play in the development of the New Testament is perhaps foreshadowed in John 19:20. As Christianity won out over the other religions of Rome, it would become a prisoner of the Roman official language—Latin.

In A.D. 382, Pope Damasus I of the Roman Catholic Church (West) asked St. Jerome to revise the existing Latin translations of the Gospels. The goal was to produce a standard, authoritative translation for the Latin-speaking Christian church, the dominant language of the Western Roman Empire.

By A.D. 405, St. Jerome, working from Greek, Hebrew, Aramaic, and Latin texts, brought together most of the Old and New Testament books to preserve the original Scriptures. For centuries, the Latin-speaking church relied on St. Jerome's translation.

In the beginning, St. Jerome's task was to produce a Latin Bible that reflected the way common people used the language. As Christianity moved west, more and more people spoke languages other than Latin. The scholarly elites and church leaders could read and speak Latin, but common people, often uneducated, could only speak their common language.

The farther Christianity moved from Rome throughout Europe, Africa, and Asia, the less and less Latin became the spoken language of the common man. As the centuries rolled on, the common man became less educated. Latin became the language of Church priests and cultural elites. The Bible was translated into other languages, but the Latin Bible and Mass remained constant until modern times.

Imagine attending a church gathering where you do not know the language being spoken. Your understanding of the Bible would be small, but more importantly, what would the result be?

The result is you being entirely dependent on people who do know that language. Yet, even if others would kindly help you understand, a barrier would always remain between you and what the Bible said unless you learned that language. Martin Luther was tasked with bringing the Bible into the common man's language in Germany. An English translation would follow years later. Locked in the Latin vault of Catholicism, the simple message of the death, burial, and resurrection of Jesus Christ (DBRJC) for the forgiveness of sin remained for centuries. The valid message of the Gospel was no longer heard from the pulpits of the Church on mass. And since the people did not know Latin, how would they know what the Bible said otherwise? The Church's priority of the four Gospels had an unintended consequence: confusion and an evident lack of understanding of the Gospel of Christ.

Many New Testament scholars know that Matthew, Mark, and Luke lack explicit teaching on salvation. Words that are common in Paul's letters about "being saved" are scarcely found in these books, even in the Gospel of John.

The lack of explicit technical language caused much confusion among the Jews who heard our Lord's teachings and the subsequent generation of readers of the four Gospels. This unrecognized fact leads to speculation by many New Testament students and disagreements about what themes, concepts, and words have "how to get saved" significance.

In other words, some look at the four Gospels and question whether Jesus really talked about "how to get saved" in his teachings. Recognizing the small amount of data in the Gospel of Mark that is explicitly about spiritual redemption in nature, one author states,

> *Thus, while the Gospel [of Mark] contains very little direct teaching about salvation, it shows salvation in action as Jesus calls human beings into a relationship of discipleship to him.*[4]

This, again, is a false conclusion about Mark's Gospel because the author assumes everything is pointing to the salvation that comes by faith in Jesus' death, burial, and resurrection for the forgiveness of sins. This confusion leads some to imply references and make false conclusions that works make a man righteous in God's eyes. One author concludes, "The Synoptics normally attach eternal life to obeying Jesus, and occasionally to trusting him."[5] Due to their assumption about the meaning and significance of Jesus' words, this is the most logical conclusion. This assumption, based on a false understanding of the teachings of Christ, forms the basis for those who think redemption comes from works—Arminianism.

Many scholars recognize a scarcity of explicit references to the Lord's death, burial, and resurrection in Matthew, Mark, and Luke. They also know that, before his crucifixion, Jesus never said explicitly that his death would be necessary so that men's sins could be forgiven. Other than the three explicit predictions of his death that we shall look at shortly, there are hints but no overt discussions of its necessity for man's spiritual salvation. There is no evidence that the Jewish crowds or the Twelve understood this. Only by looking back at the statements of our Lord with the help of after-sight do we know the potential of many of his sayings.

One clear example is found in Matthew 12:40, which highlights an exchange between Jesus and the scribes and Pharisees:

> "For just as Jonah was three days and three nights in the belly of the great fish, so will the Son of Man be three days and three nights in the heart of the earth."

Neither Matthew, Mark, nor Luke gives the reader any clue regarding the audience's understanding of our Lord's reference to Jonah. There is no evidence that the Jews understood the significance of his prediction at the time. Nor is there an explanation for why the Son of Man must die. Only after the Lord's death, burial, and resurrection did his disciples remember and then understand what he meant by many of his veiled comments.

Of the 77 occurrences of the Greek term *evangelion* in the New Testament, twelve occur in Matthew and Mark.[6] With few exceptions, modern Bible versions translate this term as "gospel." However, nothing about this term mandates this as the best English translation. No ancient church father spoke or wrote in English. Writings were either Aramaic, Greek, Latin, or Hebrew, and there are no grammatical clues to suggest when "the glad tidings," "the good news," or "the gospel" is the best translation option. Most modern translations reflect the translators' convictions about context.

In other words, the decision to translate euangélion as "gospel" is likely informed by the assumption that the term refers to DBRJC since "good news" or "glad tidings" are equally viable options. However, the historical context discussed above tells us that the term gospel was not even used to refer to Jesus' death, burial, and resurrection for the remission of sin until after Pentecost, possibly a twenty-plus-year gap. Thus, before Pentecost, we expect translators to agree that "good news" is the best option. We know that, in most modern translations, the decision to use "the gospel" (implying *the* Gospel, capital "G") was a decision guided by later developments of the term's usage. This usage is then read back into our translations of the Gospel accounts.

By the time Matthew, Mark, and Luke penned their Gospels, the term "the gospel" had come to be used in the modern sense of Jesus' sacrifice at Calvary. They would have been aware of this definition when they were writing. However, considering that (1) Jesus himself never used the term,[7] and (2) there is no OT evidence that the term was in use at that time, we would argue that this term should be translated in the Gospels in the ordinary, natural, customary sense *as it was being used at that time*: "the good news."

Must the Messiah Die?

The term "the Gospel" in its modern sense is not a meaning found in Matthew nor Mark's Gospels is confirmed by the contemporary context in which Jesus was speaking. The crowds to whom Jesus spoke did not understand that Jesus would die. Indeed, they did not know that he *had* to die. How could Jesus teach the Gospel in the modern sense of his death, burial, and resurrection without explaining this unique sense to them? There is no single example of our Lord teaching this specific topic to the multitudes or his disciples in great detail or as the fulfillment of Old Testament Scripture.

Some argue that the crowds were unbelievers to circumvent this problem. In this view, the crowds did not understand the Gospel because Jesus did not teach it. Their unbelieving status prevented them from understanding or accepting it.

It is true that, in the larger context, the idea of the death of the Messiah was not the Jewish understanding of the Old Testament Scriptures. Few, if any, first-century Jews, including Jesus' disciples, could have articulated the spiritual benefits of the death of the Messiah. If the disciples did not understand Jesus' teachings that way, why would anyone else?

When Did Jesus Start Teaching About His Death?

As we explore this idea, it's important to restate that Jesus did not teach about his death explicitly until near the end of his ministry. The Lord Jesus spoke of his death in unambiguous language on three separate occasions in the Gospels of

Matthew, Mark, and Luke. In all cases, he started making these statements only a few months before his actual crucifixion. Suppose the death-burial-resurrection-Gospel was indeed in view throughout Jesus' earthly ministry. In that case, it is all the more remarkable that John's Gospel (the most focused on "salvation" of all Gospels) does not contain any of these accounts.

The Lord Jesus made three explicit predictions of his death. Let's see what we can learn by looking at each one of these predictions. As we do, one mustn't allow the placement of the first explicit prediction in each Gospel account to prejudice the reader regarding the historical timing of the prophecy.

At first glance, based on the mid-book location of these predictions, one might conclude that the predictions occurred near the middle of the Lord's ministry. However, a closer look shows that the first half of each Gospel writer's book (Matthew, Mark, and Luke) covers approximately the first three years of Jesus' ministry. In contrast, the second half covers roughly the final six months. The fact that each writer decides to commit more than half of his book to the final six months of the Lord's ministry shows us just how important that period of his ministry was.

First Explicit Prediction of Death

We will start with Matthew 16:21–23, which reports,

> *From that time* Jesus began to show his disciples that *he must go to Jerusalem and suffer many things* from the elders and chief priests and scribes, and *be killed,* and on the third day *be raised.* And Peter took him aside and began to rebuke him, saying, "Far be it from you, Lord! This shall never happen to you." But he turned and said to Peter, "Get behind me, Satan! You are a hindrance to me. For you are not setting your mind on the things of God, but on the things of man." (emphasis added)

Four critical details should be noticed here, which directly affect the question of when he explicitly stated his imminent death, burial, and resurrection in the historical sequences of his earthly ministry.

First: The Timing of the Prediction

The phrase, *from that time,* is an important marker and has received much scholarly attention. If Jesus began teaching about his death, burial, and resurrection *from that time*, he would not have taught it before that time. Dr. Jack Kingsbury has written extensively on this unique phrase and its significance for interpreting

Matthew's timeline of Jesus' life. As a personal comment on this reality, it is interesting how some interpreters may be inconsistent. In some places, people stop and press tremendous weight on one or a few words. The same people, however, would be erratic in passing this over and shrugging it off. I recall R. C. Sproul mentioning once that you can press into single words in God's word as much as you can all 66 books.

The context of the fourth chapter of Matthew quickly demonstrates this truth. Matthew 4:17 states, "From that time Jesus began to preach, saying, 'Repent, for the kingdom of heaven is at hand.'" Whatever else our Lord said or did before John's imprisonment did not include public preaching of repentance in light of the imminent coming of the kingdom of God. This we know because the public ministry of Jesus began after the public ministry of John the Baptist. Alternative: "It seems that Matthew is using this phrase in a precise, timely manner to signify a new transition in Jesus' life and teaching." Regarding this critical phrase, David R. Bauer, in an outstanding presentation on Matthew's structure, writes that Matthew's verses "1:1, 4:17, and 16:21 are general headings which are expanded in the material that follows in each case."[8] In other words, these verses are paragraph headings.

The reader should not miss this. In Matthew 16:21, the Lord Jesus explicitly tells his disciples that his death is imminent. This is the first time Jesus has made this explicit prediction to any group, particularly his inner circle—the Twelve.

Don't Miss This Critical Point

A. T. Robertson concludes that this prediction by the Lord Jesus (Matt. 16:21, cf. Mark 8:31, Luke 9:21) occurs less than one year before his crucifixion.[9] Fred R. Coulter similarly places it as occurring between "Passover 29 AD to Passover 30 AD."[10] McGarvey and Pendleton also place our Lord's first prediction between the third Passover and our Lord's arrival in Bethany,[11] a week before his death.

Matthew places this first explicit prediction of our Lord's death immediately following Peter's explicit declaration that Jesus is "the Christ, the Son of the Living God." Matthew 16:13 places Peter's confession as "when Jesus came into the district of Caesarea Philippi." At this time, Caesarea Philippi would have been about 105 miles northeast of Jerusalem. Many think this is the farthest point Jesus went from Jerusalem. By explicitly referencing the time and place of Peter's confession, Matthew helps his readers understand that Jesus has moved into the climatic period of his earthly ministry.

We are convinced that no more than six months passed from this explicit prediction until his death on Calvary. Why is this point so important? There are several illusions that Jesus gives about his death before his last six months on Earth, but none were clear enough to form the basis of the death-burial-resurrection motif for the forgiveness of sins that came later. Jesus did not disclose the facts of his death, burial, and resurrection, nor the reason for his death, until after his resurrection. Therefore, there is no basis to see the term "the gospel" as a reference to these things before that time. Any such conclusion requires reading later developments back into Jesus' words during his earthly ministry.

Second: The Content of the Prediction

If the first statement, "from that time," speaks to the timing of when Jesus started preaching about his death, burial, and resurrection, the second statement, "began to show," demonstrates the content.

The clause "Jesus began to show" explains our Lord's actions as he started the second and final phase of his earthly ministry. The verb chosen by Matthew is distinct from the one in Mark's account, which is translated as "he began to teach them."

As the Lord Jesus turns his daily walk south toward Jerusalem, we are not Informed of his moods, attitudes, or emotional state between the first announcement of his soon-coming death and the event itself. However, the night before his death presents our Lord in great distress. It shows his understanding of the level of suffering he was about to endure beyond most human beings' comprehension.

Again, the first explicit declaration of his imminent death spoken in Matthew is marked by four realities that were going to happen. He *must* (1) go to Jerusalem, (2) suffer many things, (3) be killed, and (4) be raised.

Looking back through the lens of history, it is easy for us to supply a context that allows us to see the implicit hand of God at work here. In other words, if we believe God controls all things, then we believe none of this surprised Him. However, there is no evidence that the twelve disciples got it. We see just the opposite. Even after the resurrection of our Lord, it can still be said of the eleven disciples,

"O foolish ones, and slow of heart to believe all that the prophets have spoken! Was it not necessary that Christ should suffer these things and enter into his glory?" (Luke 24:25–26)

The Messiah needed to suffer because the prophets had predicted it. The prophets predicted God's will. Sewn in the fabric of human destiny, this unavoidable reality: glory is found at the end of the road of suffering. *A Handbook on the Gospel of Matthew* indicates:

> *Quite frequently, as here, must is used in the Gospels of a necessity imposed upon a person in the fulfillment of the divine will (see 17:10; 24:6; 26:54). Some translators have even used a phrase like "that God required that" or "that it was God's will that" to convey the full force of must.*[12]

There is no textual basis for the claim that the disciples understood this divine necessity. Jesus never implied or explicitly indicated the purpose of the events predicted in Matthew 16:21 (parallels: Mark 8:31, Luke 9:22). This is a fact that the reader must keep in clear focus. At this point, Jesus does not say that his death is necessary to forgive sin. He does not say why he must die; he only says that he must.

The death of Jesus must occur in Jerusalem. This reality lies before our Lord, who holds it in constant remembrance. This is evidenced by Luke 13:33–34:

> "I must go on my way today and tomorrow and the day following, for it cannot be that a prophet should perish away from Jerusalem. O Jerusalem, Jerusalem, the city that kills the prophets and stones those who are sent to it!"

The irony is not lost. Any prophet sent from God should be killed in Jerusalem because his message is unpopular and shows the rebellious heart of the people. It also shows their lack of understanding that killing the prophet does not stop the will of God.

The second imperative is that our Lord must *suffer many things*. In Jesus' first prediction of the coming troubles, he does not specify the elements that will contribute to his suffering.

The third imperative is that our Lord must *be killed*. Louw and Nida define the Greek verb to mean "to cause someone's death, normally by violent means, with or without intent and with or without legal justification— 'to kill.'"[13] While the Lord had spoken of "the cross" several times, it is unclear whether the disciples understood his references as metaphorical or literal.

The fourth imperative is that he be raised from the dead on the third day. In this context, being raised from the dead is a clear implication. As we read this prophetic prediction, what Jesus was saying seems clear. Yet, we must pay attention to the text and the disciples' reactions. We must not allow our familiarity with this passage to force unwarranted conclusions at this text stage.

Third: Peter's Response to the Prediction

Let's look at Peter's response, recorded in Matthew 16:22. It portrays a complete and total surprise. One is hard-pressed to explain Peter's reaction if this is not the first time he heard it. If Peter had understood that the "good news" that Jesus had taught included his death, burial, and resurrection, he would not have rebuked Jesus out of shock. Peter's response also suggests that he had no historical understanding of the need for the Son of God to die. Nor can anyone conclude that Peter received this message from Jesus as "good news." The text said that Peter *rebuked* the Lord. Peter's reaction proves this is the worst news he has ever heard.

Peter did not know *why* Jesus had to die. His ignorance can only be explained by the fact that Jesus had not yet disclosed this information to the Twelve or, even if he had, that God had blocked Peter's mind from understanding it. Nor did explaining the reason behind Jesus' death remove Peter's confusion. Typically, in a situation like this, New Testament methodology would be to insert an indication of (an explanation by way of) prophetic fulfillment. That did not happen here. The fact that the Messiah must die is prophetically detailed in the Old Testament. However, no attempt is made to clarify Peter's confusion with an Old Testament scriptural explanation, which would have been very helpful.

Peter's language is emphatic. "To rebuke" means "to express strong disapproval of someone— 'to rebuke, to denounce.'"[14] The most emphatic way to express negation in the New Testament occurs here. In a sense, Peter tells the Lord that he must suffer death in no way and under no circumstance. At this point, Peter sees no God-ordained reason for the Son of God to die. If Jesus pervasively preached his death and resurrection for the forgiveness of sin, Peter clearly must have been absent the whole time.

We see hate, sincere regret, and concern in Peter's behavior. Peter expresses the widespread belief among all Jews at the time: "We have heard from the Law that the Christ remains forever. How can you say the Son of Man must be lifted up?" Peter expresses the majority opinion among all Jews at this point in Israel's history—that the Messiah's death was not part of the Old Testament law of Moses.

Fourth: Who Heard the Prediction?

In their accounts, Mark and Luke include this first prediction of our Lord's death, burial, and resurrection. There are textual details included in Luke's account that Matthew and Mark do not give. Notice in Luke 9:21–22:

> And he strictly charged and commanded them to tell this to no one, saying, "The Son of Man must suffer many things and be rejected by the elders and chief priests and scribes, and be killed, and on the third day be raised."

The context of Luke 9:21–22 makes clear that only the twelve disciples were with the Lord Jesus when he first predicted his death. No one but the Twelve heard it, and Jesus "strictly charged and commanded them to tell this to no one" (Luke

9:21). Notice that, after telling the Twelve about his imminent death, Jesus called the crowd to come to him (Mark 8:34). The crowd did not hear Jesus' prediction.

Second Explicit Prediction of Death

Regarding Jesus' second explicit prediction of his imminent death, we place it no more than two months before the crucifixion.

Matthew 17:22–23 states:

> As they were gathering in Galilee, Jesus said to them, "The Son of Man is about to be delivered into the hands of men, and they will kill him, and he will be raised on the third day." And they were greatly distressed.

Notice the additional information in Luke 9:43–45 regarding the Lord's second prediction:

> All were astonished at the majesty of God. But while they were all marveling at everything he was doing, Jesus said to his disciples, "Let these words sink into your ears: The Son of Man is about to be delivered into the hands of men." *But they [the Twelve] did not understand this saying, and it was concealed from them, so that they might not perceive it. And they were afraid to ask him about this saying.* (emphasis added)

The context makes clear that Jesus is only speaking to his twelve disciples. Luke's account of the second prediction is short and to the point. However, he does add explanatory details. First, Luke adds that "They [the Twelve] did not understand." Luke uses this grammatical construction to express their ongoing ignorance. Luke explains why they did not understand: "It was concealed from them so they might not perceive it." The word used here is a verb that Luke uses only once in the New Testament, meaning "to hide."[15] God purposely hid the meaning and significance of the Lord's prediction from the minds of the Twelve until after his resurrection. Luke concludes with the final fact, "They were afraid to ask him about this saying."

The reader is not given the reason God prevents the Twelve from understanding. Perhaps he knew their hearts and how easily they could be impressed to desert the Lord before these frightening events unfolded. A fear of persecution or death could easily have prevented them from speaking up and asking Jesus.

Please get the points. First, only the twelve heard the prediction. Second, they did not understand what they heard. Third, God blocked their minds so they would not understand it. Fourth, they were afraid to ask Jesus what he meant. Result: complete ignorance!

The Third Explicit Prediction of Death

The third prediction is recounted in Matthew 20:17–19, where we find:

> And as Jesus was going up to Jerusalem, he took the twelve disciples aside, and on the way he said to them, "See, we are going up to Jerusalem. And the Son of Man will be delivered over to the chief priests and scribes, and they will condemn him to death and deliver him over to the Gentiles to be mocked and flogged and crucified, and he will be raised on the third day."

As best we can tell, this prediction occurs two weeks before the Lord's death. Again, the passage clarifies that "he took the twelve disciples aside." No one other than the Twelve heard what Jesus said. It would be post-Easter before the Twelve understood or talked about this information with others.

It is in this third declaration that we learn that the method of our Lord's death would be crucifixion. Both Jews and Gentiles would have a hand in the Lord's death. Luke 18:31–34 offers more insight. Luke writes,

> Taking the twelve, he said to them, "See, we are going up to Jerusalem, and everything that is written about the Son of Man by the prophets will be accomplished. For he will be delivered over to the Gentiles and will be mocked and shamefully treated and spit upon. And after flogging him, they will kill him, and on the third day he will rise." *But they understood none of these things. This saying was hidden from them, and they did not grasp what was said.* (emphasis added)

Again, please note the textual details. First, only the twelve disciples heard the prediction. Second, they did not understand what Jesus meant. Third, they did not understand because God had hidden the meaning from them. At this point, it should be clear in the reader's mind that the purpose of the Lord's death had not been communicated. This, perhaps, explains why they deserted him once his trial began.

These three accounts should dispel any notion that the "gospel about Jesus Christ" was common knowledge during Jesus's whole ministry. This is just not true. Only the Twelve heard the Lord's explicit prediction of his imminent death, and God would not allow them to understand it until after the resurrection, specifically ten days short of Pentecost.

Luke confirms this conclusion:

As they were talking about these things, Jesus himself stood among them, and said to them, "Peace to you!" But they were startled and frightened and thought they saw a spirit. And he said to them, "Why are you troubled, and why do doubts arise in your hearts? See my hands and my feet, that it is I, myself. Touch me and see. For a spirit does not have flesh and bones as you see that I have." And when he had said this, he showed them his hands and his feet. And while they still disbelieved for joy and were marveling, he said to them, "Have you anything here to eat?" They gave him a piece of broiled fish, and he took it and ate before them. Then he said to them, "These are my words that I spoke to you while I was still with you, that everything written about me in the Law of Moses and the Prophets and the Psalms must be fulfilled." *Then he opened their minds to understand the Scriptures,* and said to them, "Thus it is written, that the Christ should suffer and on the third day rise from the dead, and that repentance for the forgiveness of sins should be proclaimed in his name to all nations, beginning from Jerusalem. You are witnesses of these things. And behold, I am sending the promise of my Father upon you. But stay in the city until you are clothed with power from on high." And he led them out as far as Bethany, and lifting up his hands he blessed them. While he blessed them, he parted from them and was carried up into heaven. (Luke 24:36–50, emphasis added)

That Jesus had to open their minds to understand the connection between his death, burial, and resurrection and repentance for the forgiveness of sins is evident from Luke 24:45. The verb meaning "to open" is the single divine action necessary for the Twelve to understand both the meaning and significance of these events. That it is God's power to do so was never in question. This confirms that it was God's will for the disciples to understand these events only after they had taken place.

What may be missed by the reader is that this explicit explanation of his death, burial, and resurrection for the forgiveness of sin and their necessity occurred on the day our Lord left the earth to return to the Father in heaven. Therefore, suggesting that the term "the gospel" was invested with the meaning of the DBRJC before our Lord's departure is an abuse of Scripture. Jesus never referred to his death, burial, and resurrection as "the Gospel." The twelve disciples never understood the death, burial, and resurrection of Jesus as "the Gospel" before our Lord's death either.

Matthew 26:1 explicitly states,

When Jesus had finished all these sayings, he said to his disciples, "You know that after two days the Passover is coming, and the Son of Man will be delivered up to be crucified."

Two days before his death, the Lord Jesus stated for the last time, "The Son of Man will be delivered up to be crucified." Matthew does not record the disciples' reaction to this declaration. Mark, Luke, and John also report the events two days before Passover, but none repeat his declaration. There is no evidence that the Twelve understood the Lord's prophetic statement. They will run away at this critical hour and deny they know him. Their actions make it difficult to believe that they understood and accepted the necessity of the Lord's death, burial, and resurrection as essential for human salvation.

To what conclusion are we forced? No occurrence of the term *the gospel* as reflected in modern translation as having been explicitly spoken by the Lord Jesus can refer to his death, burial, and resurrection before the resurrection.

By confusing the gospel of the kingdom of God (the coming of the kingdom) and the gospel of Christ (the gospel of salvation due to Jesus' death, burial, and resurrection for the forgiveness of sin), many continue problems that never should have existed. Spiritual salvation requires faith. Sanctification requires faithfulness. The failure to recognize this distinction continues a firestorm of man's making.

Instead of celebrating the significance of the events culminating in Jesus' trial and eventual death, the Twelve see no spiritual or eternal value in Jesus' death. Matthew 26:56 concludes, "All the disciples left him and fled." This is hardly the behavior of men who saw and appreciated the prophetic-fulfilling significance of the DBRJC.

In the Gospel of John, on the very day Jesus was raised from the dead, John offers this editorial comment, "For they [meaning Peter and John] did not yet understand the Scripture that Jesus must rise from the dead" (NET).

CHAPTER THREE

The Good News from God

As we saw in the previous chapter, the history of the noun "gospel" and its use in the New Testament reveals that it cannot refer to the DBRJC in the Gospels of Matthew or Mark. The false conclusion that it does has caused many to misinterpret Matthew, Mark, and Luke regarding the dominant message of Jesus Christ during the inauguration of God's plans to set up a kingdom for his Son on earth in fulfillment of Scripture.[16]

Yet just 15 verses into Mark's presentation of the life and ministry of Jesus Christ, he states,

> Now after John was arrested, Jesus came into Galilee, proclaiming ***the gospel of God***, and saying, "The time is fulfilled, and the kingdom of God is at hand; repent and believe in the gospel." (emphasis added. Mark 1:14-15, ESV).

By promoting the good news about Jesus Christ as the dominant message of the Synoptic Gospels, the good news from God has effectively been forgotten or made to mean something contrary to God's original intent. In 2017, James W. Sheets, Jr. published his master's thesis entitled "The Kingdom of God: The Missing Gospel within the Gospels." In the introduction to this important essay, Sheets laments, "It would be fair to say that the Gospel of the Kingdom is the "missing" Gospel within the Gospels."[17]

God's missing "gospel" has been forced to be subservient to the Gospel of Jesus Christ instead of vice versa as Scripture intends. In other words, to lose the differences between GG and GC leaves students only one option for interpreting the word "gospel" in Matthew, Mark, and Luke: spiritual salvation.

We would add Steven R. Service's conclusion in his work, "The Lost and Forgotten Gospel of the Kingdom: A First Century Hebraic Perspective."

He writes,

> Although the contemporary Judeo-Christian world has come to identify the meaning of "gospel" narrowly with the "story of Jesus' death, burial and resurrection," this is most assuredly not what writers of the Gospels were referring to as they used the term. This is why: The Gospels make it clear, because of His disciples' inability to bear the

21

understanding that He intended to die a sacrificial death, that Jesus said nothing explicit regarding His impending crucifixion until the very end of His earthly ministry. If this point is accurate, then the "gospel" Jesus preached at the start of His ministry, could not have possibly had anything to do with the "story of His death, burial, and resurrection." The "gospel" He and others preached, in the 1st century A.D., must have been something completely different than the common definition that has been accepted by religious leaders for more than a millennium.[18]

The incorrect interpretation of the term "the gospel" at every occurrence is the trap that leads Service to this conclusion. Like so many others, he will continue to struggle with the correct interpretation of the New Testament as long as GC is thought to control its dominant message.

It may surprise some that the Greek word for salvation does not occur in Matthew. It appears only once in the disputed ending of the Gospel of Mark, four times in the Gospel of Luke, and only once in the Gospel of John. If the dominant message of Matthew, Mark, and Luke is spiritual salvation, one would think there would be many more occurrences of this family of terms.

In the previous Chapter, we demonstrated that spiritual salvation is not the dominant message of the Synoptic Gospel writers. Yet, translations contribute significantly to this false interpretation. It is unclear, nor is there a scholarly consensus, when, during the historical development of the New Testament church, the saints began to use the term "gospel" as a technical term for the DBRJC. We firmly believe that it began post-Easter Sunday.

Except for the New Living Translation,[19] all modern New Testament translations render 1 Corinthians 15:1 as "the gospel," which Paul preached. Notice Paul writes in 1 Corinthians 15:3-5,

> For I delivered to you as of first importance what I also received: that Christ died for our sins in accordance with the Scriptures, that he was buried, that he was raised on the third day in accordance with the Scriptures, and that he appeared to Cephas, then to the twelve. Then he appeared to more than five hundred brothers at one time, most of whom are still alive, though some have fallen asleep. Then he appeared to James, then to all the apostles. Last of all, as to one untimely born, he appeared also to me.

Even if we accept the notion that from Matthew 1:1 to Revelation 22:21, the term "gospel" refers to the DBRJC, a close, accurate examination of this passage implodes the whole notion. Many espouse 1 Corinthians 15:1–9 as the clearest example in the New Testament of a precise definition of the one and only Gospel of Christ, yet there are problems with this position.

A close examination of Paul's "gospel" in 1 Corinthians 15 reveals four components:

(1) that Christ died for our sins in accordance with the Scriptures.
(2) that he was buried,
(3) that he was raised on the third day in accordance with the Scriptures,
(4) that he appeared to Cephas, then to the Twelve.

Most New Testament scholars agree that verses 3–5 are a unit. There is debate about how verses 6–9 connect to verses 3–5. However, even if we ignore verses 6–9, the problem remains. Paul defines "the gospel" as a package with four components: death, burial, resurrection, and appearances. Based on the grammatical structure of 1 Corinthians 15:3–5, one cannot remove "that he appeared to Cephas, then to the Twelve" as a component of Paul's "gospel" without severely damaging the text's integrity.

Of the four elements of Paul's "gospel," what must a person believe to be declared righteous in God's sight? Must a person believe that Jesus appeared to Cephas to receive salvation?

Must a person believe that Old Testament Scripture explicitly predicts the resurrection of Jesus on the third day? If so, what Old Testament Scriptures expressly make this claim?

Paul's list clarifies that 1 Corinthians 15:1 should not be treated as a definitive statement of what constitutes "the Gospel" as we understand it today. Instead, Paul lists vital elements of his "good news" regarding the many works of Jesus Christ. As "good news," any list can include all or any of Paul's components and still be considered good news.

We have already shown that the theme of the death, burial, and resurrection of Jesus does not become part of the public discourse until the very last chapters of Matthew, Mark, and Luke, which focus on the time between our Lord's resurrection and ascension back to heaven. Thus, this motif, the dominant message of these books, does not stand the test of critical examination. With the lone exception of John the Baptist, there is no evidence that anyone at that time understood the connection between Jesus, his death, and the removal of sin (John 1:19), a fact that even John the Baptist will have second thoughts about later.

It's All About Context

While our conditioning over time has taught us that there is only one "gospel" (the one and only death, burial, and resurrection of Jesus Christ for the remission of sin), English readers must resist the temptation to assume this. To believe that every occurrence of the term *gospel* refers to the Gospel of Christ is a poor Bible study method. Hence, we insist that modern translations abandon the translation of this phrase in the New Testament as "the gospel" and utilize "the good news" in all occurrences instead. This would help the reader rely more on the context to understand the meaning rather than assuming what it means.

The One and Only Gospel?

The Gospel of John is undoubtedly the most spiritually salvation-focused book in the New Testament. If the term gospel does, in fact, refer to the DBRJC, it is surprising that it does not occur in any of John's writings.

If this is the critical term in the New Testament that describes the works of Jesus and the Gospel of John is about *the* Gospel of Christ, then why did John not use it?

In the previous chapter of this book, we showed that in the gospels of Matthew, Mark, and Luke, the term *gospel* is never shorthand for the death, burial, and resurrection motif of Jesus Christ. Instead, it refers to "the gospel of the kingdom of God."

The Beginning Message of Jesus Christ

Mark 1:14–15 reports,

> Now after that John was put in prison, Jesus came into Galilee, preaching the gospel of the kingdom of God, and saying, The time is fulfilled, and the kingdom of God is at hand: repent ye, and believe the gospel. [KJV]

Regarding these two verses and their importance, we agree with Chamblin when he writes,

> *The importance of Mark 1:14–15 can hardly be overstated. Here, for the first time, Mark records words of Jesus. These verses stand as a rubric over the whole of the ensuing Galilean ministry. Mark here presents a reader's digest of the gospel which Jesus declared throughout that period.*[20]

Please notice that final sentence again. "Mark here presents a reader's digest of the gospel which Jesus declared throughout that period." Indeed, we extend Chamblin's assertion until Jesus dies on the cross and his final 40 days on earth before his ascension to heaven. The fact that scholars have missed this critically important point is why many hold to an Arminian view of salvation, in this author's opinion.

We take this position primarily because there is no other way to interpret many passages that place conditions on following Jesus as a disciple. Since disciples do start and stop following Jesus, one must conclude that salvation can be won and lost.

Jesus came proclaiming "God's good news." We commend the New Living Translation for consistently translating the Greek word "good news." We draw this conclusion because by utilizing the phrase "the good news" rather than the phrase "the gospel," the reader is forced to use context to determine the intended meaning of the text and thus stands a better chance of recognizing the contextual difference between references to the GKG and GC.

What is the good news from God? Is it the same as the "good news about Jesus Christ"? Many New Testament scholars assume that the answer is yes. To clarify, this is the Arminian view, i.e. Arminian in the more authentic sense of works-based salvation? Since works-based salvation is unacceptable to many evangelical conservatives, some are forced to interpret difficult passages in a way that harmonizes their theological convictions. Doing this leads to errors, errors, and more errors.

Again, New Testament translations would be much more helpful if they would use the translation "the good news." This would allow the reader to discern whether this is "the good news from God," the gospel about Christ (the Gospel), or some other "good news" based on the context. For example, Luke 1:19 records a conversation between the angel Gabriel and Zechariah, the father of John the Baptist. Gabriel tells Zechariah, "I stand in the presence of God, and I was sent to speak to you and to bring you this good news." What "good news" is Gabriel talking about here? It is the birth and ministry of John the Baptist. The context forces translators to reflect the correct nuance because there is no direct focus on Jesus Christ. At this point, there is no hint of Jesus' death, burial, and resurrection motif. John the Baptist *is* the good news. We are again reminded that the word "euangélion" was an ordinary word to the Jewish people.

The same Greek verb is used in Luke 2:10, which states, "Fear not, for behold, I bring you good news of great joy." Here, "great joy" describes the good news. The great joy is the birth of "a Savior, who is Christ the Lord." At this point, there is no hint of death connected with this child. The specific acts of the child who will save the people are the unraveling story of Mathew, Mark, Luke, and John. It will be only after our Lord's resurrection that the Jews understand how the child saves his people.

In Luke 4:43, we learn that Jesus is preaching "the good news of the kingdom of God" (ESV). Luke states that our Lord said, "I must preach the good news of the kingdom of God to the other towns as well, for I was sent for this purpose." The phrase "as well" indicates that this is the message Jesus preached to all the cities of Galilee.

Here, in Luke's account, we have three distinct messages labeled as good news: (1) the birth and ministry of John the Baptist, (2) the birth of Jesus, and (3) the kingdom of God. Therefore, "to proclaim the good news" is the better verb translation, which allows the context to define what that good news is. To violate this method of interpretation is to invite error.

Mark 1:14 reports, "Now after John was arrested, Jesus came into Galilee, proclaiming the good news from God" (author's translation). Matthew 4:17 adds additional insight regarding the beginning message of the Lord Jesus. He states, "From that time Jesus began to preach, saying, 'Repent, for the kingdom of heaven is at hand.'" From that time" is a specific phrase used in Matthew that divides what went before and what goes after. In essence, the Jews did not hear Jesus announce the kingdom or call for repentance before the beginning of his ministry. This is the dominant message of Jesus' first sermon!

Luke 4:43 adds, "I must preach the good news of the kingdom of God to the other towns as well; for I was sent for this purpose." The Greek literally and emphatically says, "Because for this I was sent." Proclaiming the royal rule of God is the first dominating reason Jesus came to this earth. While there are many consequences of the Lord's first coming, it is here and in John 18:37 that it is the most precisely articulated—to announce the beginning of the reign of King Jesus over creation. While the descriptions differ, Mark, Matthew, and Luke indicate that is what Jesus teaches in his message: the good news is that, in himself, God's permanent physical manifestation of sovereign rule has arrived on earth for all to see and experience.[21]

Matthew informs us that this was the same summary message with which John the Baptist began his ministry: "Repent, for the kingdom of heaven is at hand" (Matt. 3:2). From the start of his ministry, Jesus continues the message of John the Baptist. According to Matthew's record, John and Jesus began their ministries preaching the same thing: the Gospel of God. Luke also puts this same message in the mouth of the Twelve on several occasions (Luke 8:1; 9:2, 60; 16:16; and Acts 8:12).

Finally, Luke closes the book of Acts by indicating that the apostle Paul also preached this message:

When they [the local leaders of the Jews] had appointed a day for him [Paul], they came to him at his lodging in greater numbers. From morning till evening he expounded to them, testifying to the kingdom of God and trying to convince them about Jesus both from the Law of Moses and from the Prophets.... He [Paul] lived there two whole years at his own expense, and welcomed all who came to him, proclaiming the kingdom of God and teaching about the Lord Jesus Christ with all boldness and without hindrance. (Acts 28:23, 30–31)

Paul had a two-point sermon: (1) the kingdom of God and (2) Jesus, i.e., the king and his sovereign administration. Rather than maintaining this vital distinction, most New Testament readers have dissolved any separation in the content of these messages and blended them to such a degree that the dominant message of the Synoptic Gospels is wholly lost. Jesus physically manifested the royal rule of God on earth ("the Gospel of God") and left an open invitation for his disciples to join the membership of his coming leadership council during his thousand-year reign on earth.[22]

The Chronology of Jesus' Ministry

The chronology of the initial events of our Lord's ministry can be a bit confusing, given the differences in the accounts of the four Gospel writers. Those who attempt a harmony of the Gospels agree that, for the most part, Jesus began his public ministry "after John was arrested." The importance of John's ministry to that of Jesus is critical. Luke 16:16 states,

Until John the Baptist, the law of Moses and the messages of the prophets were your guides. But now the Good News of the Kingdom of God is preached, and everyone is eager to get in. (NLT)

There is debate about where to draw the line regarding John's inclusion or exclusion from the age of "the good news of the kingdom of God is preached." Perhaps, Luke 7:28 is helpful. It asserts that "among those born of women none is greater than John. Yet the one who is least in the kingdom of God is greater than he." Thus, the age of Law and Prophets ended with John, a prophet in the tradition of Elijah. Bock concludes,

The fundamental point here is that the kingdom period, one that followed the ministry of John, is so great that the least who share in it are greater than the greatest prophet of the older era. One gets the clear impression from this text that the period of the kingdom of God begins with Jesus' ministry and message.[23]

Therefore, two eras transitioned with the John the Baptist and Jesus ministries. Since Matthew summarizes the message of John the Baptist and the Lord Jesus Christ as "Repent, for the kingdom of heaven is at hand" (John = Matt. 3:2 and Jesus = Matt. 4:17), a comparison is easy to make. Matthew's assertion that John and Jesus preached the same message allows us to look for the defining traits of this message.

Both Matthew 3:1–12 and Luke 3:1–20 give the most extended descriptions of the ministry and message of John the Baptist. Matthew begins his account with the simple explanation that "John the Baptist came preaching in the wilderness of Judea." Having skipped John's miraculous conception, Zechariah's discipline, and John's earliest excitement at being in the presence of our Lord while he was in the womb of his mother (which Luke details), Matthew states the essence of John's message: "Repent, for the kingdom of heaven is at hand."

Whatever else "to repent" might come to mean in the New Testament era, at this early juncture, it had nothing to do with what would come to be known as "the Gospel." The average reader generally sees this New Testament concept of repentance as unbelievers turning from their past sins and accepting Jesus Christ as Lord and Savior. In the Gospels, most see this as a necessary step to "get" saved so they can go to heaven. However, to see repentance as a step toward being saved is to read a modern concept back into the biblical period, identical to what we explained with the word "gospel.

What Is the "Good News of God"?

Matthew states the heart of our Lord's message. Mark 1:14–15 defines the essential components of this message as follows: (1) the time is fulfilled; (2) the kingdom of God is at hand; (3) repent; and (4) believe in the gospel (of the kingdom). According to Mark, this is "the good news from God." The KJV reflects manuscript evidence supporting the longer phrase "the good news of the kingdom of God" here. While evidence favors the shorter reading, the more extended reading does appear in the Gospel of Luke on three separate occasions (4:43, 8:1, and 16:16).

While there is some debate about the origination of Matthew's use of the clause "the good news from God," there is no confusion regarding its origination in Luke.[24] Since both passages refer to the same message, we can take Luke's version, "proclaiming the good news of the kingdom of God," as the fullest expression of the content of the Lord's original message.

Now, for fear that the reader misunderstands the message, we need only to continue reading. Mark 1:15 says the content of the Lord's statement: "The time is fulfilled, and the kingdom of God is at hand; repent and believe in the gospel." Mark 1:15 begins with the phrase "and saying that." This indicates the content of what Jesus said.

Most scholars generally agree upon the basic structure of verse 15. Some focus on the grammatical components: two declarations ("the time is fulfilled" and "the kingdom of God is at hand") and two commands ("repent" and "believe in the good news").[25]

A Closer Look at the Gospel of God

The phrase "the Gospel of God" occurs seven times in the New Testament, with one variation in 2 Corinthians 11:7. Only Mark 1:14–15 explicitly defines "the gospel from God." Sadly, New Testament scholarship consistently interprets any use of the term "gospel" as a reference to the DBRJC. This is not the case in Mark 1:14, but it is consistently interpreted as such by the overwhelming majority of New Testament scholars.

In this view, every occurrence of the term "gospel" in the New Testament references the DBRJC. Many New Testament scholars read later developments back into our Lord's words and subsequently draw erroneous conclusions that are not warranted.

Besides Paul, the apostle Peter uses the phrase "the gospel of God" in 1 Peter 4:17–19:

> For it is time for judgment to begin at the household of God; and if it begins with us, what will be the outcome for those who do not obey the gospel of God? And if the righteous is scarcely saved, what will become of the ungodly and the sinner?

Just as John the Baptist's message (the good news from God) was a message of impending judgment for which only the righteous (in actions) will escape, we find the same elements in 1 Peter 4.

Just as in John the Baptist's preaching, "the gospel of God" is a warning message to change behavior from evil to righteous to avoid the coming judgment. As is consistent from Adam to Abraham to David to the Twelve to us, faith in the promise of God brings righteousness from God.

It is a choice to be in a state of repentance or unrepentance. "Those who do not obey" are those who are unrepentant. It would be a significant error to conclude that Peter draws a line between believers and unbelievers here. He puts the line between those who repent and those who do not. Thus, the people of God can be among the unrepentant! What will happen to each group is not the same, but there will be negative consequences.

Paul uses the phrase "the gospel of God" (Rom. 1:1) to summarize God's extraordinary work in Jesus that entails far more than just the DBRJC. He uses it to refer to both spiritual and physical salvation and the privilege of ruling with Christ during his coming sovereign administration on earth. Because Paul's "good news" includes both, it would be better to utilize "the good news" as the translation in Romans 1:1 to ensure that the phrase is contextually determined and not automatically assumed.

The "Gospel" Preached in Rome

Recognizing the gospel of God as more than an announcement of the benefits of the DBRJC for the forgiveness of sin explains why Paul could write in Romans 1:8–15:

> First, I thank my [Father] God through [the Son of God] Jesus Christ for all of you, because *your faith* is proclaimed in all the world. For [the Father] God is my witness, whom I serve with my spirit in the Good News of his Son [Jesus Christ], that without ceasing I mention you always in my prayers, asking that somehow by [the Father] God's will I may now at last succeed in coming to you. For I long to see you, that I may impart to you some spiritual gift to strengthen you—that is, that we may be mutually encouraged by *each other's faith*, both yours and mine. I do not want you to be unaware, brothers, that I have often intended to come to you (but thus far have been prevented), in order that I may reap some harvest among you as well as among the rest of the Gentiles. I am under obligation both to Greeks and to barbarians, both to the wise and to the foolish. So I am eager to preach the good news [of God] to you also who are in Rome. (translation and emphasis mine)

After celebrating the Roman church for their faith being "proclaimed in all the world" and hoping that "we may be mutually encouraged by each other's faith," Paul expresses his eagerness "to preach the gospel [of God] to you also who are in Rome." Paul has restated his intent to visit the believers in Rome, given "that I [Paul] have often intended to come to you [the church in Rome] that I may reap some harvest among you as well as among the rest of the Gentiles."

Here is a prime example of how distinguishing between GG and GC makes sense of passages that otherwise do not if "gospel" only refers to GC. The "gospel" Paul longed to preach was not the "gospel about Christ" relating to spiritual salvation. As Paul states in Romans 1:8 and 12, the church in Rome was already celebrated for its faith, which "is proclaimed in all the world."

Paul longed to preach the gospel *of God*, which warns men of the coming judgment and the coming kingdom, and Paul wants to be included as part of the leadership. Salvation by grace through the atoning sacrifice of Jesus on the cross is an essential first step, but the gospel of God is more comprehensive.

The failure to appreciate this difference guarantees confusion and frustration in many texts. The merger of these two completely different messages results in twisting, squeezing, and forcing passages to conform to a false doctrinal conclusion.

Translations that cause both the articular noun *to evangelion* and the infinitive *euangelizesthai* to mean "the Gospel," i.e., the DBRJC for the forgiveness of sin, exacerbate the problem.

Again, this is precisely why we advocate the translation "the good news" at every turn and that the immediate context be used to define its content. The good news about Jesus Christ provides the basis for God's impartation of righteousness to a sinner, but "the good news from God" promises inclusion in the leadership of the coming physical manifestation of the royal rule of God on earth.

Understanding the two sets of "good news" is particularly critical when a New Testament author uses the term *gospel* without a qualifier. Paul begins the book of Romans with an explicit declaration that he was "set apart for the gospel from God." Schreiner is correct that Paul's "good news" "cannot be limited to the initial decision to join the Christian community," i.e., get saved. "The good news from God" insists that perseverance to the end is necessary for "deliverance – deliverance for unbelievers at the sheep and goat judgment; and deliverance for believers at the bema seat judgment. Perseverance is a demand of "the good news from God" and not "the good news about Christ."

In our view, perseverance is a sanctification issue rather than a salvific one. Salvation is a faith issue alone, while sanctification is a faithfulness issue.

Paul uses the phrase "the gospel of God" again in Romans 15:16. He exalts being "a minister of Christ Jesus to the Gentiles in the priestly service of the gospel of God." He celebrates "what Christ has accomplished through me to bring the Gentiles to obedience." Notice that the fulfillment of "the ministry of the gospel about Christ" makes Paul successful in bringing "the Gentiles to obedience."

The phrase "the gospel of God" occurs thrice in 1 Thessalonians 2. In the face of persecution by the Jews, Paul reminds the Thessalonians that "the gospel of God" produced results—their obedience. In proclaiming "the gospel of God," Paul and his team did not violate God's commands with wrong motives, i.e., flattery to make money or to seek the honor of men. To not infringe upon the call of "the gospel from God," Paul was committed to giving rather than receiving.

Paul concludes 1 Thessalonians 2:1–16 with the sobering reality: "But wrath has come upon them at last." Paul is speaking of those:

who killed both the Lord Jesus and the prophets; drove us out and displease God and oppose all mankind by hindering us from speaking to the Gentiles that they might be saved—so as always to fill up the measure of their sins.

God will punish bad behavior with his wrath. Again, we see that a discussion of "the gospel of God" occurs in a context where behavior should be designed in light of the eschatological coming of God's wrath. The gospel of God warns humankind (both believers and unbelievers alike) that living a penitent life will ensure safety from God's imminent wrath. Unbelievers must be penitent, and believers must be repentant.

Mark 1:15 defines the good news of the kingdom of God as consisting of three primary pillars: (1) the time is fulfilled; (2) the kingdom of God is near; and (3) repent and believe the gospel [of the kingdom of God]. We shall explore each pillar separately in the following three chapters.

CHAPTER FOUR

What Time Is It?

Many people may find it challenging to accept that Jesus' references to "the gospel of God" do not refer to the Gospel about Christ. Yet, because most New Testament students believe there is only *one* gospel, this view has become widely accepted and ingrained in the thinking of many in the church because of a misinterpretation of Paul's statement in Galatians 1:6-7.

In Mark 1:15, the most straightforward and precise definition of the good news (gospel) of God occurs. Mark records that Jesus' first sermon listed three essential pillars of the GG. The first pillar concerns the unique age that began with the birth of the Messiah—Jesus, the Son of God and Son of Man. Jesus stated, "The time is fulfilled" (Mark 1:15a). The Gospel of Mark, alone, restates the declarative statement of Jesus, but without any illuminating commentary. What time is Jesus referring to here? When did it begin? Did those who heard Jesus speak immediately understand what he meant? Is this new period strictly Jewish, or is there a broader audience that includes Gentiles?

The permanent physical manifestation of God on the earth marks the new age. To better help the reader understand the uniqueness of this age, Luke re-purposes the Nazareth rejection narrative[26] of Jesus because it contains the most explicit self-identification by Jesus that he is the long-promised Jewish Messiah. Jesus makes this identification by quoting Isaiah 61:1–2a. What is so special about Luke's account is not just *where* Luke places it in the chronological timeline of our Lord's forty-two-month-ministry but also the purposeful rearrangement of Isaiah's passage, which make two critical points: (1) the four attributes of the messianic age for mankind and (2) the dawning of the age of God's favor.

A Journey Back Through History

Israel's Old Testament history concludes with the book of Nehemiah, which is gloomy. For their disobedience, the tribes of Israel would be enveloped by a shroud of darkness—no prophet from God would declare "the word of the Lord" for four centuries.

Yet, the tribes were not left without hope. The prophet Malachi recorded that the re-appearance would break this darkness of "Elijah the prophet," who would come at a time to inspire family reconciliation and turn away the wrath of God.

Malachi 4:5–6 states,

> "Behold, I will send you Elijah the prophet before the great and awesome day of the LORD comes. And he will turn the hearts of fathers to their children and the hearts of children to their fathers, lest I come and strike the land with a decree of utter destruction."

The tribes were likely looking for a quick fulfillment of this promise, yet this was not to be. The promise would go unfulfilled for 400 years. Then, suddenly and without warning, an angelic visit would break the silence and tell of the imminent birth of a son of David. This child's birth and early life—the Lord Jesus—receive little attention in the biblical record. It is with Jesus' public ministry that his biographies begin.

Matthew, Mark, Luke, and John situate the beginning of Jesus' ministry by showing that Old Testament prophecy was fulfilling. Matthew and Mark agree that the public ministry of Jesus begins "after John the Baptist was arrested."[27] We might then describe this transition from John's preaching to Jesus's preaching as a ministerial "handing off of the baton." The difference is that John's ministry pointed to Jesus, and Jesus' ministry pointed to his sovereign administration. Each Gospel writer describes Jesus' "breaking into history" in a unique way. All insert Jesus as God's solution for Israel's problem (silence), but each does it differently.

Breaking of Silence in Luke

While Matthew and Mark position Jesus as the fulfillment of Old Testament prophecy, Luke takes this further. He frames the Lord's earthly ministry as inaugurating a decisive turning point in human history. Luke's remarkable exposition of the event, only hinted at in Mark 1:15a, teaches us that this is an important time. In Luke, we learn what time it is!

This remarkable exposition revolves around Luke's use of Isaiah 9:1. Matthew utilizes Isaiah 9:1 to focus on the time for light to dispel the darkness for God's people that began during their exile. Luke is more ingenious. He defines "the time is fulfilled" with theological precision. To build his case, Luke utilizes Isaiah as well. He takes an event from the life of Christ as the basis for his assertion: the time when Jesus reads Isaiah 61:1–2a in the synagogue at Nazareth and proclaims that the hearers are witnessing its prophetic fulfillment. This event (called "the rejection event" by scholars) likely occurred near the midpoint of Jesus' ministry. However, unlike Matthew/Mark, who records this event chronologically, Luke chooses to record it at the front end of his account, which is out of chronological order.

The Point of the Rejection Narrative

The Gospels record that Jesus walked into the synagogue of Nazareth, opened the scroll, and read Isaiah 61:1–2a aloud, which describes the prophesied Messianic ministry's essential components. Jesus then puts down the scroll. He sits down, looks at his audience, and says, "Today, this Scripture has been fulfilled in your hearing." His audience was stunned. There was no mistaking what he was saying. Jesus had just announced that the benefits of the long-awaited Messiah were to be fulfilled in him. He was ushering in the temporal royal rule of God (and, by extension, the eschatological Jubilee) foretold by the ancient prophets. These long-awaited events brought the promise of God's kingdom on earth and freedom for God's people. They were also temporal events that were separate and distinct from the spiritual salvation that would come from Jesus' sacrifice at Calvary.

While the average modern reader might not fully appreciate the impact of Jesus' announcement, it would not have been lost on Jesus' hearers. The persecution of the Romans against the Jewish people made them yearn for the kingdom rule that Scripture promised through God's long-promised messiah.

The nation of Israel had been waiting for hundreds of years to see the fulfillment of Old Testament prophecy. The Jews in Nazareth did not reject Jesus because they had a problem with Scripture being fulfilled. They rejected Jesus because they had a problem with him being the one to do it.

It did not help that Jesus confronted his hometown crowd with their unbelief. When Jesus announced that these prophecies were "fulfilled in your hearing," it set the Jews of Nazareth's teeth on edge. They literally wanted to kill Jesus.

At this point, nothing about the rejection narrative suggests that the people of Nazareth understood that the death of Jesus would benefit them or mankind, in general, for spiritual salvation. They wanted to kill Jesus for their own reasons.

Let's start with Luke's decision to move the rejection story to the beginning of his narrative account of Jesus' ministry. This decision differs from Matthew and Mark, who placed it in the correct chronological sequence. Luke's decision reflects the significance he places upon Jesus' announcement in his development of the storyline of the Lord's ministry. By doing so, Luke uses the narrative to frame the rest of his Gospel, i.e., an outline of the Lord's ministry.

Anderson summarizes:

> *Whereas in Mark's record the Rejection episode is placed just before the Galilean ministry draws to its close (Mark 6:1–6), and whereas Matthew presents it as the climax of the Galilean ministry (Matt. 13:53–58), in Luke's Gospel it appears to stand as a preface to the public ministry.*[28]

Luke sees that the Lord Jesus defined his ministry in light of Isaiah 61:1–2a as so significant that he places this story out of chronological sequence. There is much debate among NT scholars about why Luke rearranges the sequence to put this sermon at the beginning of his account. Our view is that, whereas Matthew and Mark tell us what the Lord preached, Luke additionally tells us *why* he preached.

Luke 4:16–19 indicates that Jesus' ministry on earth would be a prophetic fulfillment of Isaiah 61:1–2a. Luke alone records,

> And the scroll of the prophet Isaiah was given to him. He unrolled the scroll and found the place where it was written, "The Spirit of the Lord is upon me, because he has anointed me to proclaim good news to the poor. He has sent me to proclaim liberty to the captives and recovering of sight to the blind, to set at liberty those who are oppressed, to proclaim the year of the Lord's favor."

Most New Testament scholarship holds that Luke 4:18–19 = Isaiah 61:1–2a reflects the Septuagint, the Greek translation of the Old Testament, rather than the Hebrew Masoretic text. One basis for this claim is that "24 out of 26 words in the quotation are identical with the Greek translation of the Old Testament."[29] Even more significant is the Septuagint's utilization of the verb "to proclaim good news" to translate the Hebrew verb, which means "to bear tidings."

In this passage, Jesus quoted Isaiah 61:1–2a and announced, "Today this Scripture has been fulfilled in your hearing." Many New Testament scholars see this section in Luke as a summary of his ministry and message during his time on earth.[30] One author writes, "Luke 4:16–30, because of its placement at the beginning of Jesus' public ministry, functions in a programmatic way for the whole of Luke.[31] By "programmatic," scholars suggest summarization. In other words, everything Luke records—the entire summation of Jesus' ministry in his eyes—is wrapped up in this one statement: "Today this Scripture [the physical manifestation of God on earth] has been fulfilled in your hearing." Hagner writes, "This key pericope is virtually a programmatic or summarizing statement for the importance of living according to the righteousness of the newly arrived kingdom."[32]

David Hill also supports the programmatic thrust of Luke 4:16–30. He writes, "The position of the pericope is due to its character as an 'advance' notice of the essential message of Luke's theology."[33] If this is true, we should find throughout the rest of Luke's writings a constant reference to "the gospel of God" and the crucial time (the time of the royal rule of God) in which we live and, indeed, we do. Luke's account focuses heavily on the essence of this period in time—the arrival of Messiah Jesus and the evidence of such, including his ministry and the accompanying miracles. Luke allows our Lord's reading of Isaiah 61:1–2a to define the time.

A closer examination of Luke 4:18–19 reveals several peculiarities. Notice,

> "The Spirit of the Lord is upon me, because he has anointed me to proclaim good news to the poor. He has sent me to proclaim liberty to the captives and recovering of sight to the blind, to set at liberty those who are oppressed, to proclaim the year of the Lord's favor."

Now notice how the verses read from Isaiah 61:1–2:

> The Spirit of the Lord GOD is upon me, because the LORD has anointed me to bring good news to the poor; *he has sent me to bind up the brokenhearted,* to proclaim liberty to the captives, and the opening of the prison to those who are bound; to proclaim the year of the LORD's favor, *and the day of vengeance of our God; to comfort all who mourn.* (emphasis mine)

The first peculiarity concerns what is left out of the quote of Isaiah 61:1–2: the clause "he has sent me to bind up the brokenhearted." Second, the latter half of verse two drops off: "and the day of vengeance of our God; to comfort all who mourn." A clause from Isaiah 58:6 is added: "to proclaim good news to the poor." What is the significance of these details? We do not have enough information to determine whether the Lord Jesus introduced the clause from Isaiah 58:6 into his sermon or whether Luke introduced it to explain his original intent. Either way, it is safe to conclude that its inclusion helps Luke's readers to fully comprehend the Lord's intent for reading from the Isaianic text.

What we do know is that a comparison of the resultant text in Luke 4:18–19 reveals a clear intent of the Author/author to emphasize "the ministry of release" begun by Jesus. Notice:

> "The Spirit of the Lord is upon me, because he has anointed me to proclaim good news to the poor. He has sent me to proclaim liberty to the captives and recovering

of sight to the blind, to set at liberty those who are oppressed, to proclaim the year of the Lord's favor."

Jesus the Eschatological Jubilee

By adding Isaiah 58:6, Luke emphasizes that the Lord Jesus was sent by God "to proclaim *liberty* to the captives" and "to set at *liberty* those who are oppressed." Our English term "liberty" captures the Greek term "release" or "liberty." Luke uses this term more often than any other NT writer, which suggests its importance to Lukan theology.

More importantly, the Greek term translates the Hebrew term (meaning "release" or "emancipation"), which occurs in Isaiah 61:1, and yôbēl transliterated "jubilee," which appears in Leviticus 25:10. Thus, with Jesus's ministry, a new era begins.

While Matthew and Mark generally reference our Lord's rejection in Nazareth (Matt. 13:53–58, Mark 6:1–6), Luke references the event and details the content of his message. Our analysis reveals the Lord's core message as he went from synagogue to synagogue, teaching.

Luke picks up on the Lord's reference to Isaiah 61 because of the significant theme Isaiah developed there. We agree with Bergsma, who states, "Isaiah 61 is the text that represents the most widely recognized biblical allusion to the jubilee outside of the Pentateuch."[34]

The Jubilee is central to God's character—so central that God's decision to allow the enslavement of Judah to the Babylonians for 70 years is directly attributed to Judah's disregard for keeping 70 Jubilee years. 2 Chronicles 36:17–21 sketches the consequences of this failure. It records,

> Therefore, he brought up against them the king of the Chaldeans, who killed their young men with the sword in the house of their sanctuary and had no compassion on young man or virgin, old man or aged. He gave them all into his hand. And all the vessels of the house of God, great and small, and the treasures of the house of the LORD, and the treasures of the king and of his princes, all these he brought to Babylon. And they burned the house of God and broke down the wall of Jerusalem and burned all its palaces with fire and destroyed all its precious vessels. He took into exile in Babylon those who had escaped from the sword, and they became servants to him and to his sons until the establishment of the kingdom of Persia, to fulfill the word of the LORD by the mouth of Jeremiah, until the land had enjoyed its Sabbaths. All the days that it lay desolate it kept Sabbath, to fulfill seventy years.

God enslaved his people for 70 years to reclaim the land's right to have a sabbath rest.[35] Judah did not learn the lesson, for there is no report of the people celebrating or honoring a Sabbath-year rest after returning from Babylon.

Daniel 9:2 confirms that Judah's freedom came exactly 70 years later. Daniel 9:2 records, "In the first year of his reign, I, Daniel, perceived in the books the number of years that, according to the word of the Lord to Jeremiah the prophet, must pass before the end of the desolations of Jerusalem, namely, seventy years."

By referencing Isaiah 61:1–2a, Jesus again brings God's value of the Jubilee to the forefront. What our Lord references briefly, Luke develops extensively. Having set the basis for his theological assertion by quoting Isaiah 61:1–2a and 58:6, which emphasize "release," Luke develops this theme throughout the rest of his Gospel and the book of Acts. By quoting two passages with this same idea in Isaiah, Luke establishes the controlling theme of our Lord's message. He came to demonstrate God's eschatological "release" (or jubilee) for his people.

The most explicit NT reference to the Jubilee is in Luke 4, where Jesus applies the Jubilee proclamation of Isaiah 61 to himself.[36] Thus, Jesus is God's Jubilee for his people. The Isaiah quote ends with our Lord's assertion that liberty has come in the year of God's favor. Jesus, God's anointed one, brings "good news" of freedom or release to the poor, blind, captives, and oppressed. Through his ministry, Jesus proves that physical and spiritual realities are present in his proclamation.

What Jesus alludes to in brief, Luke expands significantly. The noun *release* occurs 17 times in the New Testament. Ten of these occurrences are divided equally between Luke's Gospel and Acts. Except for Luke 4:18, which quotes Isaiah 58 and 61 and emphasizes the consequence of sin's enslavement of mankind, the rest of the noun occurrences in these two books accompany the noun *hamartia* = sin. Jesus proclaims man's release or liberty from sin. In every occurrence, the term for "sin" is plural. Thus, the ministry of Jesus announces that both the enslavement to sin and the punishment associated with that enslavement are ended. Those who believe in God's message and messenger are free, liberated, and released to live as God intended.

This is not just a release from sin but also a much larger package of liberties that includes bondage, oppression, physical sickness, demonic possession, and poverty in the coming kingdom. Jesus released the power of God in his people and community in a way that his listeners had never seen before.

In his Gospel, Luke explicitly states that Jesus Christ's ministry and message inaugurated a new era for God's people—the year of God's favor—a favor marked by freedom from sin's awful consequences.

CHAPTER FIVE

What Is the Kingdom of God?

Mark 1:14–15

> Now after John was handed over (to prison), Jesus came into Galilee, shouting out loud the good news from God, by saying, "The time is fulfilled, and *the sovereign administration of God is at hand;* repent and believe in the good news (from God)."
> (author's translation, emphasis added)

Our Lord's message of the good news from God primarily concerns two things: timing ("the time is fulfilled") and royal rule ("the sovereign administration of God").

In the previous chapter, we discovered that our Lord's definition of "the good news from God" involved a decisive turning point in human history—a dividing line between the age of the Law and Prophets and the kingdom of God. We now focus on the second declarative statement: "The kingdom of God is at hand."

George E. Ladd concludes: "[T]he Kingdom of God was the central message of our Lord's ministry."[37] As his ministry progressed, Jesus made several explanatory comments about the nature of the kingdom of God. Of particular importance is Luke 17:20–21, which records a dialogue between Jesus and the Pharisees regarding the nature of the kingdom. Luke reports,

> Being asked by the Pharisees when the sovereign administration of God would come, he [Jesus] answered them, "The sovereign administration of God is not coming in ways that can be observed, nor will they say, 'Look, here it is!' or 'There!' for behold, the sovereign administration of God is in the midst of you."
> (author's translation)

This passage has been greatly misunderstood by both liberal and conservative scholars alike. Confusion about the nature of the kingdom of God naturally leads to confusion about what the Lord Jesus meant when he talked about it. The Pharisees' misunderstanding did not end with their generation.

We see the same in the Church Fathers and modern scholarship. Yet, Gerald F. Hawthorne argues that "Luke 17:20–21 contains the most explicit statement of the *essential* nature of the Kingdom anywhere recorded in the words of Christ.[38]

The Jews saw the coming rule of God over Israel as the next major event on God's calendar. To them, breaking off the yoke of Rome would have been the best evidence that the kingdom had arrived, and that is precisely what they were expecting. We continue to see this expectation even in the disciples' question just minutes before our Lord ascended to heaven a few days before Pentecost. They asked, "Lord, will you at this time restore the kingdom to Israel?" (Acts 1:6).

However, the Lord Jesus made clear to his audience that the sovereign administration of God would not first evidence itself by overturning earthly governments. In fact, the rule of God has been on earth since before creation itself. Just because God has limited the overt manifestation of his sovereign rule does not mean he is not in control. What was in question was the degree to which man is involved in God's rule on earth and the evidence thereof. How much of God's authority does man have, and what overt manifestations can we see that proves it?

Our Lord asserts that "the sovereign administration of God is already among you." Scholars have wrestled with the meaning of the final clause of verse 21. Modern translations offer several possible ways to translate the original Greek, including "within you" (ESV), "among you" (NLT), and "in your midst" (NET).

Because the sovereign administration of God involves jobs that men and women must earn, we agree with Colin H. Roberts' conclusion regarding the meaning of this key phrase as "with you, in your possession, if you want it, now."[39] Roberts, an Oxford papyrologist, suggested that the expression means "within your reach."[40] G.R. Beasley-Murray cites Roberts with approval regarding this translation.[41] Bock also makes room for this sense.[42] Professor H. J. Cadbury, writing for the *Christian Century,* also endorses Roberts' thesis, saying that so understood "the sentence means...the availability, the accessibility, the opportunity, of the kingdom."[43]

Our Lord's essential points were that the sovereign administration of God cannot come where it already exists and that participation in the rule of God remains open to men and women, i.e., leadership positions remain to be filled.

This is the critical stage where disciples must try to earn the right "to participate in the sovereign administration of God." *The Exegetical Dictionary of the New Testament* suggests "kingdom" or "reign" as the translation of the Greek noun for kingdom.[44] It concludes:

> *In secular Greek the meaning of the word alternates between a functional sense—royal sovereignty, monarchy, royal dignity, royal office—and the geographical sense of kingdom or realm.... Both meanings are also represented in the NT: sometimes the reference is to kingdom or realm (e.g., Matt 4:8; Mark 6:23; 13:8; Rev 16:10), and sometimes to royal sovereignty (e.g., Luke 19:12, 15; Rev 1:6; 17:12).[45]*

A Greek-English Lexicon of the New Testament and Other Early Christian Literature also agrees with this assessment.[46] In their lexicon, Louw and Nida draw a similar conclusion.[47] Therefore, lexically speaking, the Greek term for kingdom can have a functional or a geographical sense. How a particular author uses the term for a specific passage must be discerned from the immediate context.

In reference to God, one will need to pay close attention to the context. Most New Testament scholars agree that when coupled with God in the NT, the term kingdom "is essentially an abstract noun referring to the 'rule' or 'kingship' of God."[48] I. Howard Marshall would add,

> *[T]here is a growing agreement that the phrase KG should be taken to refer primarily to God's sovereignty rather than to the realm over which he is sovereign.[49]*

As far back as 1902, Dalman wraps both the Old Testament and the New Testament kingdom concept in this conclusion when he writes,

> *[T]hat in the OT, Jewish literature, and in Jesus' teaching, "malkut, when applied to God, means always the 'kingly rule,' never the kingdom,' as if it were meant to suggest the territory governed by him."[50]*

In 1988, Joel Marcus published an excellent article entitled "Entering into the Kingly Power of God," in which he concludes,

> *Relying especially upon exegesis of Jewish parallels and of the first category of Jesus' sayings, many twentieth century interpreters have claimed that the predominant meaning of malkûtā'/basileia in Jesus' teaching is "reign," "rule," "sovereignty," "dominion," "kingly power" rather than "realm."[51]*

Even more insightful is Marcus' assertion that the New Testament emphasis is not so much on the fact of God's reign but the exercising impact of this reign on his creation, something he calls "a 'dynamic' interpretation." He writes,

> *In speaking of a "dynamic" interpretation of basileia, I depart somewhat from Dalman, whose favorite translations of malkut/basileia are "sovereignty," "kingly rule," and even "theocracy." These translations are not explosive enough; they portray God's basileia as the abstract fact that he rules, rather than the force of his personal self-assertion that manifests his kingship by overpowering the resistance to it in the earthly sphere.[52]*

A Better Translation

While Dalman's favorite translation is "sovereignty," and Marcus prefers "kingly power," we prefer "sovereign administration." By using "the sovereign administration of God," we emphasize the active role God is now playing in the day-to-day running of this world through his Son Jesus, the God-Man, and those men and women the Father gives to him. The phrase "the sovereign administration" focuses on the rulers of the coming physical manifestation of God's rule on earth. When God manifests his physical presence, it will no longer be through burning bushes, storm clouds, fire on mountaintops, or other inanimate objects. Instead, it will be through the God-Man and those whose extreme faithfulness is rewarded with the honor to rule with him.

The sovereign administration of God refers to Jesus' administration or government.[53] All disciples are greatly encouraged to pursue participation in the leadership of the coming kingly rule.

Perhaps nothing has contributed more to the confusion regarding the meaning of the phrase "the kingdom of God" than the New Testament use of the verb "to enter." Matthew (19:24), Mark (9:47, 10:23, 24, 25), Luke (18:24, 25), John (3.5), and Paul (Acts 14:22) all employ a Greek infinitive with a preposition to express this idea. The clause "to enter the sovereign administration of God" occurs nine times in the New Testament.[54] As English speakers, we use the verb with several nuances. For example, we say that a person enters a building, room, or car. When we do, we understand intuitively that the person moved from one physical location to another.

We also used the verb "to enter" in a non-local sense. We have all probably been approached about "entering" a raffle contest to win a prize at one time or another. In this sense, we pay a fee, write our information on a form, or are given a ticket with a matching number as the other part is dropped into a spinning drum. Without any need for explanation, we understand that, by doing so, we have "entered" the contest. Yet, we do not personally get inside the drum! We could have just as easily said that we agreed "to participate" in the contest.

This latter sense is found in the New Testament. As the second possible nuance of the Greek verbal εἰσελθεῖν εἰς, Arndt, Danker, Bauer, and Gingrich, in their lexicon, suggest that New Testament usage supports the sense "to enter into an event or state, of pers[on] come into someth[ing] = share in someth[ing], come to enjoy someth[ing]."[55] Louw and Nida suggest a similar sense: "[t]o begin to experience an event or state—' to begin to experience, to come into an experience, to attain.'"[56]

In the NT, we see this usage as the best way to explain how one enters into a state or condition in specific contexts. Matthew 25:21 promises the faithful a reward.

That reward is defined as "entering into the joy" of their master. The joy of one's master is a state of being. One can share, experience, or participate in another's joy. Therefore, we offer the following translation of Luke 17:20–21:

> Being asked by the Pharisees when the sovereign administration of God would come, he answered them, "The sovereign administration from God is not coming in ways that can be observed, nor will they say, 'Look, here it is!' or 'There!' for behold, the sovereign administration is available to you now."

God's Four-Step Plan

God the Father has assigned the God-Man several responsibilities to carry out in order to manifest a physically sustained appearance on the earth of Almighty God.

Phase 1 was the physical manifestation of himself through Jesus to combine the rule of heaven (God) and earth (Man) under Jesus, the God-Man. This phase was accomplished through the life, death, and resurrection of Jesus Christ, which is reflected in John 10:30, 33–38. Phase 2 was to reward with the kingship of the earth the faithful God-Man whose completion is evidenced by his seat at the right hand of the throne of God (Heb. 12:2). Phase 3 is the building of a kingdom leadership team, first from his first-century disciples, then from the larger class of disciples called the church. Only the most faithful will receive an invitation to be included in the ruling class of the God-Man's rule on earth during the Millennium. Inclusion in this leadership team is not automatic. One must earn it by faithfulness. Phase 4, the final phase of the Father's plan, culminates with the God-Man delivering all authority back to the Father for all eternity-future (1 Cor. 15:24).

Seeing the intended meaning of the phrase "the kingdom of God" as the sovereign administration of God through the physical manifestation of his authority on the earth is critical. This alone explains the multiple conditions expressed in the New Testament for how a disciple attains elite status in the coming ruling class with Jesus Christ. Understanding the nature of the sovereign administration of God will protect the intent of the New Testament and prevent false doctrine. Otherwise, one will have to believe in works salvation. There is no other way to harmonize the good news from God and the good news about Jesus Christ.

Acquiring elite status in the ruling class is a matter of sanctification, not salvation. The recognition of this one fact would have prevented the whole lordship salvation debate from arising in the first place (and robbing many of their confidence in the good news of salvation by faith alone). Participation in the sovereign administration of God is a reward gained by faithfulness. If one proves unfaithful, he or she will not participate in it. In essence, he or she will not rule with Christ.

Suffering: A Condition to Rule

That this is true is easily proven. Luke writes that the apostle Paul exhorted his Asian converts to suffer so they could "participate in the sovereign administration of God." Notice in Acts 14:21–22, Luke writes,

> When they had preached the gospel to that city and had made many disciples, they returned to Lystra and to Iconium and to Antioch, strengthening the souls of the disciples, encouraging them to continue in the faith, and saying that through many tribulations we must earn participation in the sovereign administration of God. (author's translation)

Acts 14:22b should remove any doubt in the readers' mind that the prerequisite of suffering "to participate in the sovereign administration of God" makes the attainment of salvation (the forgiveness of sin) outside the intent of this passage. Scripture nowhere teaches that a person must suffer to be saved from sin.

Paul had already preached to these converts, and they had expressed faith in Jesus Christ before Paul's final exhortation. The disciples in Lystra, Iconium, and Antioch were already faithful believers. Yet Paul calls for suffering so that they might "participate in the sovereign administration of God."

Whatever else the clause "to participate in the sovereign administration of God" might mean, it cannot be the attainment of personal salvation from sin. To receive the righteousness of God, one must believe in the Lord Jesus Christ, period. There is no other condition. One does not have to suffer to be saved from sins.

One may suffer because he or she is saved, but no one obtains salvation by personal suffering. Otherwise, one must determine how much suffering one must experience to be saved. Could one know if he or she has suffered enough to be saved before death? Is one type of suffering better than another? The questions are endless!

In no less than six separate passages in the New Testament, the clause "enter the kingdom of God" occurs. Mark 9:47 has the clause once. Mark 10:23–25 has it three times (with parallels in Matthew 19:23–24 [twice] and Luke 18:24–25 [twice]). John 3:5 and Acts 14:22 both have the clause once. In each case, there is a conditional prerequisite beyond simple faith "to enter the kingdom of God."

As we shall see, one can participate in God's coming rule on the earth, but not as a member of the elite ruling class. This conclusion allows for the possibility that one's faithfulness will determine rewards and that unfaithful believers will not share in kingdom leadership or other blessings associated with the Lord Jesus and his earthly rule.

Faithfulness: A Condition to Rule

Matthew 21:43 makes it crystal clear that one's participation in the sovereign administration of God can be lost due to unfaithfulness. The text states,

> "Therefore, I tell you, the sovereign administration of God will be taken away from you and it will be given to a people producing its fruits." (author's translation)

In context, the Lord Jesus is addressing "the chief priests and the elders of the people," who were questioning him about his authority (Matt. 21:23). In response, Jesus asks a question: "The baptism of John, from where did it come? From heaven or from man?" He did not answer theirs because the Pharisees and elders were unwilling to answer his question.[57]

Please notice that this was not the end of the matter. The Pharisees and elders' unwillingness to believe "the baptism of John" was from heaven (and, therefore, required their submission and repentance) had tremendous ramifications. The Lord rebuked them in response to their hard-heartedness (Matt. 21:31b–32).

He pronounced that their participation in "the sovereign administration of God" would be taken away and given to a people producing its fruit. Participation in royal leadership of the coming rule of God is what the Jewish leaders lost.

In our Lord's denunciation of the Jewish leaders, he states, "Truly, I say to you, the tax collectors and the prostitutes go into the kingdom of God before you." Instead of the usual verb, the text has another verb: "go before, lead the way, lead forward."[58] Matthew 21:31b says, "Truly, I say to you all, "The tax collectors and the prostitutes are going ahead of you all into the sovereign administration of God."

If the phrase "the kingdom of God" means "the sovereign administration of God," as we suggest, then how can the tax collectors and prostitutes go ahead of the Jewish leaders? The road to reigning with Jesus begins with repentance (Matt. 3:2). Man must reverse his behaviors to comply with heaven's rules. He or she commits to living under the manifested authority of God. He or she obeys the good news from God. The reason repentant tax collectors and prostitutes can gain participation in the sovereign administration of God while the Pharisees and Jewish leaders are losing it is because of the difference in their states of repentance. The self-righteous religious leaders see no need for repentance, while the humble sinners gladly receive the grace of God and live in light of it. One repents, and the other does not. It is that simple. This is precisely what John the Baptist was teaching, too!

Piety: A Condition to Rule

Mark 10:23-25 indicates that the rich will have great difficulty participating in the sovereign administration of God. Notice,

> Jesus looked around and said to his disciples, "How difficult it will be for those who have wealth to participate in the sovereign administration of God!" And the disciples were amazed at his words. But Jesus said to them again, "Children, how difficult it is to [earn] participate in the sovereign administration of God! It is easier for a camel to go through the eye of a needle than for a rich person to [earn] participation in the sovereign administration of God." (author's translation)

These comments of the Lord Jesus follow a question-and-answer session with a rich young ruler, who asks, "What must I do to inherit eternal life?" This question could potentially have been asked out of ignorance. Perhaps the young man did not know that righteousness comes by believing the promise of God as Abraham had done. Perhaps by "inheriting eternal life," the young man was asking how to get his sins forgiven so he could go to heaven when he died. However, if he asked the wrong question because he did not understand the issues correctly, it seems incumbent on the Lord Jesus to have set him straight. Thus, the Lord Jesus might have said, "Your question is incorrectly phrased. If you want to know how to get your sins forgiven so you can go to heaven, then you must believe in the Gospel." Plain and simple.

Yet, this is not what Jesus did. First, he told the rich young ruler to work hard by keeping all the commandments. Then, after the young man reported that he had kept all the commands from his youth, the Lord Jesus doubled down on his work ethic. He told the young man to work even harder by giving all his wealth to the poor and follow him, presumably to death. Even if the young man had been capable of keeping the law perfectly, it still would not have resulted in his salvation. Even if the young man had sold all that he had and given the proceeds to the poor, it still would not have resulted in his sins being forgiven. So why did the Lord Jesus give this young man what appears to be misleading information? If you bring a modern and limited understanding of the "gospel," you can conclude the wrong thing.

To "inherit eternal life" does not mean believing in Jesus for sin's forgiveness. Notice that the Lord equated his question with "participating in the sovereign administration of God." The young man asked Jesus: "How can I ensure that I will be a ruler in the coming sovereign administration of God?" Jesus informed him that he could have wealth in the next by rejecting worldly pleasure in this life. Building great treasures in heaven now ensures that one will be included in the coming sovereign administration from heaven.

Sadly, the young man walked away, which greatly saddened our Lord. The level of commitment necessary to receive great rewards in heaven was more than he was prepared to do. Thus, he will have no position of authority in God's coming sovereign administration.

Nor will he inherit the riches of King Jesus. This rich young ruler is the poster child for the third soil in the parable of the sower.[59] The deceitfulness of riches choked the Word and thus bore no fruit.

Spiritual Salvation: A Condition to Rule

John 3:3 and 5 say that one must be born of the water and the Spirit to see/enter the kingdom of God. In what are the only occurrences of the phrase "the sovereign administration of God" in all five of John's books in the New Testament, John 3:3, 5 is unique. Please pay close attention to Jesus' remarks that John repeats in this passage. In a dialogue with Nicodemus about the need for a second birth, Jesus educates him about the *spiritual* birth. The reader must understand that Nicodemus not only believes in God's existence but also in God's promises. He understands the basics and can dialogue with Jesus as long as the conversation utilizes language he understands. However, just like many modern readers, there is a bit of confusion once the language changes from what he is accustomed to. So, the Lord changed the reference point.

First, the Lord states, "Unless one is born again, he cannot see the sovereign administration of God." In the second statement, he says, "Unless one is born of water and the Spirit, he cannot participate in the sovereign administration of God." At face value, one would think the two verses mean the same thing.

It would appear that verse five defines verse three. To be born of water and the Spirit explains how one is born again. To be born of water is repentance, as evidenced by the ministry of John the Baptist, which the Pharisees and the elders refused to do because of their self-righteousness. To be born of the Spirit is to receive righteousness by faith in the promise of God. We know what "to participate in the sovereign administration of God" means. Is it the same as "to *see* the kingdom of God?"

The verb *to see*, which means "to see with the eyes," appears more than 400 times in the New Testament, with a human always doing the seeing. Of the seven different nuances listed by Louw and Nida, "to experience" is among them, specifically "to experience an event or state, normally in negative expressions indicating what one will not experience."[60] This is a crucial detail.

According to Louw and Nida, John 3:36 should reflect this meaning in the translation. Instead of the ESV's translation, "Whoever believes in the Son has eternal life; whoever does not obey the Son shall not see life," a better reflection of the intended meaning is, "Whoever does not obey the Son shall not experience life." John 8:51 and Hebrews 11:5 also have this meaning. Remember, this is one of the same meanings for "to enter," which is our basis for the conclusion that "to participate" or "share in" is the intended meaning of the phrase "enter the kingdom of God." Without the new birth, one cannot participate or share in the sovereign administration of God.

The Jews had among them those who believed that their Jewishness ensured their inclusion in the coming Davidic kingdom. Like everyone else we meet in the stories about Jesus, Nicodemus is ignorant about the exact nature of the kingdom of God and needs instruction about how it comes and who will participate in it. Thus, if the new birth is necessary to participate in the sovereign administration of God, then it certainly cannot be *equal to* the sovereign administration of God. It is the difference between sanctification and salvation.

Paul writes in 1 Corinthians 6:9–10 that only faithful believers will inherit the kingdom of God. He writes,

> Or do you not know that the unrighteous will not inherit the kingdom of God? Do not be deceived: neither the sexually immoral, nor idolaters, nor adulterers, nor men who practice homosexuality, nor thieves, nor the greedy, nor drunkards, nor revilers, nor swindlers will inherit the kingdom of God.

Sadly, to maintain their theological systems, some New Testament teachers must maintain that Paul is here speaking of unbelievers. Their belief system does not allow unfaithful believers to suffer adverse consequences at the Bema Seat judgment. Thus, all conditional passages in the NT either speak of people who were once saved but were subsequently lost again or were never saved and only appeared to be believers on the outside.

Losing Ruling Status

Perhaps no church in the New Testament was as gifted as the church in Corinth. It had all the gifts of the Spirit.

They had the best Bible teachers in church history: the apostles Paul and Peter, along with Apollos, Aquila, and Priscilla. Yet, they had more problems than many other churches combined. A study of 1 and 2 Corinthians reveals various issues emanating from the wicked culture of the city of Corinth. Just as today, Christians were living with one foot in the world and one foot in the church. Thus, they were being called out by the apostle Paul. Some were acting in ignorance. Others were acting in willful disobedience. All were in serious need of repentance.

Finally, Paul encourages the Thessalonians about their worthiness to participate in the sovereign administration of God because they were suffering. He encourages them by saying,

> This is evidence of the righteous judgment of God, that you may be considered worthy of the sovereign administration of God, for which you are also suffering—since indeed God considers it just to repay with affliction those who afflict you, and to grant relief to you who are afflicted as well as to us, when the Lord Jesus is revealed from heaven with his mighty angels in flaming fire, inflicting vengeance on those who do not know God and on those who do not obey the good news of our Lord Jesus, [2 Thess 1:5-8]. (author's translation)

Acts 14:22 indicates that Paul admonished new churches to accept suffering as their ticket to participation in the sovereign administration of God. The Thessalonians received Paul's instructions and were commended for their suffering. Through suffering, the Thessalonians become *worthy* of this honor. The fundamental truth of the New Testament is that suffering for righteousness results in a gain of rewards (Matt. 5:10–12; Luke 22:28–30). Notice that belief in Jesus Christ alone does not make one worthy. To be worthy, one must add suffering!

Already and Not Yet

The physical manifestation of God's sovereign administration on earth has already begun. It began with Jesus Christ's life and ministry. Some New Testament scholars recognize this "already/not yet" aspect of this time. D. Nah explains,

> *"Already/not yet" is the view that the kingdom of God has already been inaugurated in the person and ministry of Jesus Christ but will not reach consummation until his return in glory.[61]*

Dr. Darrell Bock has argued to our satisfaction the validity of the "already/not yet" understanding of our Lord's ministry. In his book *Progressive Dispensationalism*, Bock writes,

> *The biblical characteristic of viewing events from a variety of perspectives shows us that one can make points from "both-and" perspectives without denying either side of the present-future relationship. It is possible to get fulfillment "now" in some texts, while noting that "not yet" fulfillment exists in other passages. In fact, in some texts, fulfillment can be initial or partial, as opposed to being final and total. As a result, one can speak*

of inaugurated eschatology without denying either what the Old Testament indicates about a future, earthly kingdom or what the New Testament asserts about the arrival of the kingdom as part of fulfillment in the first coming of Jesus. To call such eschatology inaugurated is only to say the process of fulfillment has commenced; there is more—even much more—to come . . .. "Already-not yet" teaching links the plan of God into a unified whole. It allows one to see both continuity and discontinuity in the outworking of God's promises.[62]

Bock's argument for seeing an "already/not yet" perspective in the writings of Luke/Acts is detailed in his article "The Reign of the Lord Christ" in the book *Dispensationalism, Israel, and the Church: The Search for Definition.*[63]

Bringing Sovereign Rule to Earth

Since God has ruled all creation from heaven since before creation itself, in what sense has the sovereign administration of God come to earth? How is God's physical earthly rule different from God's sovereign rule from heaven?

During the age of the Law and Prophets, God primarily worked the miraculously supernatural from heaven. The only exceptions were the prophets who, through God, exercised supernatural power on earth. As reflected in the Old Testament, no single man or woman who was not a prophet or prophetess exercised sovereign power on earth except for a few judges.[64] Outside of the prophets Moses, Elijah, Elisha, and Samuel, there were no other miracle workers during the age of Law and Prophets.

However, Jesus came preaching that the physical manifestation of God's sovereign administration had come near. He announced that God's lordship over his creation was no longer being exercised from heaven exclusively by God or his messengers. It was now exercised on earth through anyone who believes in God, including his Son.

Jesus made clear that the evidence of the physical manifestation of God's sovereign administration on earth is the ability of his disciples to set aside natural law. Luke 9:1-2 report,

And he called the twelve together and gave them power and authority over all demons and to cure diseases, and he sent them out to proclaim the sovereign administration of God and to heal. (author's translation)

Subsequently, Luke 10:1–2a and verse 9 also report,

After this the Lord appointed seventy-two others and sent them on ahead of him, two by two, into every town and place where he himself was about to go. And he said to them... "Heal the sick....and say to them, 'The sovereign administration of God has come near to you." (author's translation)

Luke 10:17 reports, "The seventy-two returned with joy, saying, 'Lord, even the demons are subject to us in your name!'" The evidence of God's active sovereign rule on the earth is the ability of a disciple of Christ to exercise power over all demons and to heal all diseases. A disciple can be a man or a woman. This is the age of the physical manifestation of the sovereign rule of God on earth.

Sadly, New Testament scholarship has largely failed to understand the intended meaning of our Lord's proclamation in Luke 10:9. The focus has been primarily on the verb's meaning, often translated as "to come near" or "approach."

Dr. Bock is correct when he writes,

There is currently a large debate about the meaning of the term. Does the perfect tense here of the verb "to draw near" mean "to approach," or does it mean "to arrive"?

Louw and Nida suggest "come near"[65] as the basic meaning of the term. Thus, scholars debate the influence of the stative aspect on the meaning. As with many theologically significant truths in the Bible, scholars often create more problems than they solve trying to explain the intended meaning. The stative aspect (perfect tense) conceives of the action by the language user as reflecting a given state of affairs.[66] The resultant state is primary in the mind of the speaker.

On several occasions, the verb has contextual qualifying details that help establish our Lord's intent. Whether the sovereign administration of God has "approached" or "arrived" is scholarship debating peripherals. We are inclined to follow Guelich's conclusion when he states, "Thus the Kingdom of God has "come into history," the appointed time "has been fulfilled," even though the full appearance is yet to come.[67] This interpretation supports the "already/not yet" aspect of God's sovereign administration. God's sovereign rule has come to earth, and men and women can now participate in it.[68]

CHAPTER SIX

Repent and Believe the Good News

(the Sovereign Administration of God)

> Now after John was handed over (to be imprisoned), Jesus came into Galilee, shouting out loud the good news from God by saying, "The time is fulfilled, and the sovereign administration of God is at hand; change your behavior and believe in the good news from God." (Mark 1:14–15, author's translation)

The final component of the good news about God's sovereign administration is a two-part command. Literally, the clause reads, "You all change your behavior and believe in the good news [from God]" (author's translation). Just as John the Baptist (whose message is synonymous with our Lord's message), repentance is the primary responsibility of the people of God and should result from belief in God's good news.

As with so many other salvation truths, the verb "to repent" has taken on a life of its own that often bears no relationship to a specific text. Just as the interpretation of the term "gospel" suffers from bad Bible study methods, "repentance" is no longer contextually defined. It is given a generic meaning in every place it occurs in the New Testament. Regardless of translation, there is no distinction offered between what the term meant during the ministry of Jesus and what it came to denote during the ministry of Paul and the apostles or our modern age.

The following paragraph, taken from *The Bible Knowledge Commentary* published by the faculty of Dallas Theological Seminary, is typical. It says,

> *Repentance and faith (belief) are bound together in one piece (not temporally successive acts). To "repent" (metanoeō; cf. Mark 1:4) is to turn away from an existing object of trust (e.g., oneself). To "believe" (pisteuō, here pisteuete en, the only NT appearance of this combination) is to commit oneself wholeheartedly to an object of faith.*

55

Thus, to believe in the good news meant to believe in Jesus Himself as the Messiah, the Son of God. He is the "content" of the good news (cf. v. 1). Only by this means can one enter into or receive (as a gift) the kingdom of God (cf. 10:15).[69]

John D. Grassmick, who wrote the commentary on Matthew in the *BKC*, makes the same mistakes as most New Testament conservative scholars. First, in their attempt to protect salvation by faith alone, "repentance" and "belief" are equated. Second, they insist that "to repent" means to turn away from an object of trust. Third, they instruct that to "believe in the gospel" means to believe that Jesus is the Messiah, the Son of God, and that this meaning occurs from the very first day of our Lord's ministry. Fourth, they teach that Jesus is the "content" of the gospel of God in Mark 1:15. Lastly, they assert that one is guaranteed "entrance" into the kingdom of God by believing in Jesus. Not a single one of these conclusions is true.

Adopting this conclusion leads to contradictions in the writings of Paul, Peter, and John. The command "to repent and believe" is assigned a non-contextual meaning to reach this conclusion. To maintain the false position that every occurrence of the term must refer to the death, burial, and resurrection of Jesus Christ for the forgiveness of sin, the language of the text must be made to say that which one would not normally conclude. Similarly, "to repent" must mean changing one's mind about Jesus Christ, which results in personal salvation from sin. Contextual meaning is ignored to foster this prejudiced notion.

Grassmick states that only by repentance and belief in Jesus "can one enter into or receive (as a gift) the kingdom of God." As is typical, he insists that "repentance" and "faith" are opposite sides of a coin. Yet, it must have escaped Grassmick's notice that Jesus told the chief priests and the Pharisees, "The kingdom of God will be taken away from you and given to a people producing its fruits" (Matt. 21:43). If the kingdom of God can be taken away, then in no sense can it be equated with spiritual salvation. Unless that is, one is willing to conclude that God can take away personal salvation for unfaithfulness, which is precisely what one must conclude if one follows Grassmick's logic.

Historical Evaluation of the Term: Repentance

The first recorded occurrence of the verb "to repent" in the New Testament falls from the lips of John the Baptist in Matthew's Gospel. Did the people instantly understand what John meant? The answer is an emphatic *no*. Luke 3:10 makes that abundantly clear. We know this because the people asked him, "What then shall we do?" Naturally, such a direct question warrants a straightforward answer. If the modern definition of repentance is accurate, why did John not simply respond, "Believe in Jesus, the Christ, and be saved"?

We describe John the Baptist's call for repentance in Luke 3:10–14 as a reformation of behavior. Certain behaviors were to stop, and other behaviors were to start. The new behavior would put one in a proper relationship with God at his coming wrathful judgment. John's call to "repentance" is aimed at the children of God (not a bunch of unbelievers in the modern sense of the word). Few, if any, Jews at this particular point did not believe in the God of Abraham, Isaac, and Jacob and were not waiting for His deliverance from Rome.

With this in mind, perhaps we should abandon the term "repentance," given that it has acquired a meaning not intended by its first usage in the New Testament. No one, certainly not John the Baptist, attached the meaning "the death, burial, and resurrection of Jesus Christ" to this word. This would be a later development that must not be read back into the synoptic record.

Consistent with Old Testament usage, a call to change one's behavior to turn away the wrath of God was never the first command to "unsaved folk." It is a command to the people of God. Even our English term "repent," with its prefix "re," inherently acknowledges that the person must have previously been penitent to re-pent.

A study of the Old Testament reveals that everyone followed no clear prescription when called to turn to God. It was not a twelve-step program. What one did depended on what one needed to avoid.

Commands to God's People in the OT: *turn*

The term most consistently used throughout the Old Testament to describe the commanded behavior of God's people when they had abandoned righteous living is the Hebrew verb *shúv*. Regarding this verb, David A. Lambert summarizes that none of the other Old Testament terms for the concept had

> *The number of attestations or the suggestiveness to stand as the appointed articulation of "repentance" in the Hebrew Bible. That honor has been reserved for a peculiar phrase, "return [shuv] to YHWH," whose range proves far more impressive, from the early, eighth-century prophets, to Jeremiah, to the deuteronomistic writings, and on to a variety of postexilic texts.[70]*

Mark J. Boda, in his book *Return to Me*, an in-depth theological study of the doctrine of repentance in both the Old and New Testaments, draws similar conclusions to Lambert regarding the meaning of the verb *shúv*. He writes,

Within Hebrew the most common word associated with repentance is the verb šûb (qal; 'turn', 'return').[7] One can 'turn' (šûb) to God or righteousness,[8] as well as 'turn away' (šûb) from evil.[9] This root is employed in the hiphil [Hebrew verb where the subject causes the action] to refer to turning away from evil[10] as well as to the action of one to prompt repentance in another.[11] The noun šûbâ refers to repentance in Isaiah 30:15.[12]
[71]

More than one verb or noun is used in the Old and New Testaments to express the idea of "turning." There is also the recognition that repentance is expressed through images, forms, and concepts. Regardless, one is called to either make an internal shift or a change in external behavior, or both. Regardless, the term is applied to believers or those considered to be the children of God. Neither the Hebrew nor the Greek term is used to refer to an unbeliever who becomes a converted member of the children of the Jewish God.

The New Testament Usage

Boda highlights a similar finding in the New Testament. In Acts 26:16–20, interpreters must force themselves not to rush to judgment. While it is typical of New Testament students to label Paul's Damascus Road experience as his conversion, one must not frontload the meaning of "conversion." If by "conversion," one means spiritual salvation by faith in Jesus Christ, a grave error will result.

If we believe that Abraham was made righteous because of his faith in the promise of God, and we very well should because it is true (Gen. 15:6, Rom. 4:3), then Paul certainly believed in the God of Abraham and operated his life based on belief in the promises God made to Abraham, Isaac, Jacob, and King David. Paul's conduct before encountering Jesus Christ on the Damascus Road is consistent with Old Testament saints. His ignorance about who Jesus Christ was should not be interpreted to mean that Saul (eventually changed to Paul) was unsaved in the later New Testament sense. To do so is to commit a severe injustice to biblical theology.

In Acts 26:12–18, the apostle Paul rehearses his Damascus Road experience for the last time. After Saul asks a question about the identity of the one who appeared to him, the Lord Jesus states,

> "I am Jesus whom you are persecuting. But rise and stand upon your feet, for I have appeared to you for this purpose, to appoint you as a servant and witness to the things in which you have seen me and to those in which I will appear to you, delivering you from your people [the Jews] and from the Gentiles —to whom I am sending you to open their eyes, so that they may turn [*epistrepho*—to turn-infinitive] from darkness to light and from the power of Satan to God, that they may

receive forgiveness of sins and a place among those who are sanctified by faith in me.' "Therefore, O King Agrippa, I was not disobedient to the heavenly vision, but declared first to those in Damascus, then in Jerusalem and throughout all the region of Judea, and also to the Gentiles, that they should repent and turn to God, performing deeds in keeping with their repentance."

That Paul was ignorant of Jesus Christ's identity does not mean that Paul was unsaved, for Abraham was ignorant of the actual identity of Jesus, but he was still declared righteous. In Paul's case, his "repentance" changed his understanding and behavior toward Jesus. He came to believe in Jesus Christ as the fulfillment of all Old Testament promises, which required his repentance regarding his previous unbelief. However, "to repent" does not mean that one changes his or her mind about Jesus Christ in all cases.

Nor does it mean "to get saved" automatically. Instead, accurately understanding the call to repent and turn to God requires careful attention to the audience that receives the command. For the children of God (Israel), repentance is very different than for the Gentiles, who did not know God. The call for repentance by Jesus in connection with the "gospel" of God in Mark 1:15 must not include the post-Easter call to repentance for the Gentiles. Rather, the good news from God commands repentance by the Jews in light of their rebellious living.

The "At Hand" Nature of the Kingdom of Heaven

Why does the "at hand" nature of the kingdom of heaven require repentance = a call to return to God? Both John the Baptist and Jesus preached the same message. The message of Matthew 3:2, 4:17, and Luke 3:18 is summarized by saying, "He [John] preached good news to the people." Matthew 3:6 indicates that the people "were baptized by him [John the Baptist] in the river Jordan, confessing their sins." The reader must understand that neither the Lord Jesus nor John the Baptist called people to repent of their sins and believe in the Lord Jesus so they could go to heaven. Rather, John declared that in association with the physical manifestation of God on earth would be the manifestation of God's wrath that could be avoided only by living a righteous life.

John the Baptist told the people that one coming after him "will baptize you with the Holy Spirit and fire" (Matt. 3:9). Who or what John meant is not made clear, and certainly not one, if any, of his listeners fully understood when and how the fulfillment would come.

This fact is borne out in the Book of Acts. In Acts 19:1–7, the apostle Paul encounters disciples of John the Baptist more than 25 years after they received the baptism of John. These disciples were utterly ignorant of the good news about Jesus Christ or that the baptism of the Spirit had come. Yet these devotees to John's teaching were serious people. Notice,

> And it happened that while Apollos was at Corinth, Paul passed through the inland country and came to Ephesus. There he found some disciples. And he said to them, "Did you receive the Holy Spirit when you believed?" And they said, "No, we have not even heard that there is a Holy Spirit." And he said, "Into what then were you baptized?" They said, "Into John's baptism." And Paul said, "John baptized with the baptism of repentance, telling the people to believe in the one who was to come after him, that is, Jesus." On hearing this, they were baptized in the name of the Lord Jesus. And when Paul had laid his hands on them, the Holy Spirit came on them, and they began speaking in tongues and prophesying. There were about twelve men in all.

Paul's encounter with these disciples of John the Baptist is insightful. His question, "Did you receive the Holy Spirit when you believed [John's message]?" is somewhat surprising. One would think Paul's first question would have been an inquiry about their faith in Jesus. Did their response to John's message bring their salvation? The text is unclear regarding what Paul expected them to have believed, but there is no doubt that Paul saw these folks as "believers," if by "believers," we mean men who had received the righteousness of God.

Their response, "No, we have not even heard that there is a Holy Spirit," is even more interesting. First, in Matthew 3:11, John is reported to have promised, "I baptize you with water for repentance, but he who is coming after me is mightier than I, whose sandals I am not worthy to carry. He will baptize you with the Holy Spirit and fire." Now, we were not privy to every sermon John preached. We don't know whether John said the same thing daily or whether what we read in Matthew and Luke are summary conclusions.

What exactly these twelve men heard from either John the Baptist or the disciples of John the Baptist (see John 1:35; Mark 2:18) is not certain. However, if we take their words at face value, it seems very odd that they would not have heard John's promise of a coming baptizer with the Holy Spirit. Equally, the text does not identify the men as Jewish (and thus knowledgeable of the Old Testament Scriptures) but as disciples of John. Hence, the idea that they had never heard of the "Holy Spirit" seems incredible.

Perhaps Acts 19:2 does not correctly express the Greek text's original intent, as the ESV reflects. The way Luke describes the men's response to Paul is difficult to understand. Some have suggested the verse should read, "We did not so much as hear whether the Holy Spirit is given." In this reading, the men are not expressing ignorance of the Holy Spirit but ignorance regarding his coming.

We agree with H.A.W. Meyer, who asserts,

> *The existence of the Holy Spirit at all cannot have been unknown to the men, because they were disciples of John and John's baptism of water had its essential correlate and intelligible explanation in the very baptism of the Spirit—even apart from the O.T. training of these men, according to which they must at least have been aware that the Holy Spirit was something existing—ἔστιν (to be so accented) must necessarily be taken as.... No, we have not even heard whether the Holy Spirit is there (already present on the earth). Accordingly, they still remained ignorant whether that which John had announced, namely, that Jesus would baptize with the Holy Spirit, had already taken place, and thus the πνεῦμα ἅγιον had become present.*

Thus, what the men were ignorant of was not the existence of the Holy Spirit but the fulfillment of John's promise that "He will baptize you with the Holy Spirit and fire." It is a little under 2,500 miles from Jerusalem to Ephesus. In our modern way of thinking, we expect news to travel fast. Yet, this was not the case in ancient times. Israel was a small nation with very little international importance. Not much would have made the front-page news coming out of Israel for the rest of the world during Jesus' day.

"The Gospel" in the modern sense was not known or taught by Jesus Christ's followers until after his death, burial, and resurrection. The essence of John the Baptist's message is not to believe in Jesus Christ's death, burial, and resurrection for the forgiveness of sins so one can go to heaven. Neither Jesus nor John the Baptist taught such a thing explicitly during the entirety of their ministries.

Indeed, some of John's Jewish audience members would have included those who believed in God and his promises but who needed revival due to God's silence for more than 400 years. It is an assumption on the part of many that John the Baptist was distinguishing between saved and lost people, i.e., believers and unbelievers, disciples and non-disciples. The assumption is that John calls unbelieving Jews to faith in God for salvation from sin and that one of the steps required is repentance. This assumption is false.

The Object of John's Message

Matthew and Luke indicate that John had a harsh tone of judgment to his message. Matthew 3:7 says that John's tone pointed at the Pharisees and Sadducees. Luke begins by saying that John spoke "to the crowds that came out to be baptized by him." There is no basis to limit the audience to Jews only. Neither is there any reason to restrict it to nonbelievers. Matthew 3:5–6 asserts, "Then Jerusalem and all Judea and all the region about the Jordan were going to him, and they were baptized by him."

Upon closer examination of John's message, we discover two metaphors of judgment that signal the need to repent immediately. The soon-coming judgment is an expression of God's wrath: "Who warned you to flee from the wrath to come?" The word "wrath" speaks of God's indignation/anger against sin. When told of the imminent outburst of God's wrath on the earth, Luke 3:8–14 reports that members of the crowds asked, "What then shall we do?" Again, as we alluded to earlier, if the issue is the lostness of their souls, we naturally expect an answer detailing our Lord's role in salvation. However, John the Baptist points not to a lack of salvation but to a lack of good fruit. Again, if the modern Gospel were in focus, one would think John would have pointed out the problem of a lack of faith in Jesus. Instead, the type of repentance John is calling for is a behavioral reformation.

Told not to depend on their Abrahamic lineage to escape the coming wrath, John describes the kind of actions that can avert God's wrath. He urges the crowds:

> "Whoever has two tunics is to share with him who has none, and whoever has food is to do likewise." Tax collectors also came to be baptized and said to him, "Teacher, what shall we do?" And he said to them, "Collect no more than you are authorized to do." Soldiers also asked him, "And we, what shall we do?" And he said to them, "Do not extort money from anyone by threats or by false accusation, and be content with your wages."

John's answers ought to remove any possibility that he is preaching about Christ's provision of his life for man's sin. There is nothing explicit or implicit here about needing faith in Jesus to forgive your sins. Rather, John the Baptist focuses on behavior. The good news from God calls upon men to bring their behavior in line with living under God's rule.

If John had been talking about the provision for man's sin, we would have expected him to outline the plan of salvation in a post-Easter sense. Rather, just as with Abraham, he called on the people to believe God's promise: "repentance for the forgiveness of sins." Belief in this promise is evidenced in their behavior. Salvation came to Abraham and the Jews in Jesus' day and to us in the same way: belief in the promise of God—the content of the promise from man's perspective changes.

There does not seem to be any confusion on the part of the people about John's message or their necessary response. Equally, there is no basis for anyone to claim that the general masses thought Jesus was God or able to forgive sins. The reader must remember that Jesus had just begun his public ministry with a message he labeled "the good news from God." Repentance must be seen in the light of this message.

The call to repent is found in both the Old and New Testaments. On one occasion, Jesus remarked, "The men of Nineveh will rise up in the judgment with this generation and condemn it because they repented at the preaching of Jonah, and indeed a greater than Jonah is here" (Matt. 12:41). On two separate occasions, our Lord will speak of Assyrian cities that either did or would have responded to the call for repentance: Nineveh (Matt. 12:31) and Tyre/Sidon (Lu 10:13).

Who were the Assyrian people? Why did God demand repentance or destruction of their great city? Were the Ninevites once a people of God? Does national repentance imply a previous relationship between God and those called "to turn back to God"?

If these questions had as their primary subject the children of Israel, then the answer to these questions would be an emphatic yes! However, no less emphatic is the fact that all nations owe their existence to the God of the Bible. Psalm 86:9 declares, "All the nations you have made shall come and worship before you, O Lord." In the same way that all the nations shall be blessed through Abraham (Gen. 12:3), all the nations will draw his wrath for their wicked rebellion (Psalm 2:1–3) against his law (Gen. 9:1–7). There will be an eschatological punishment of all the world's nations, but for now, God extends grace. Nineveh is one such recipient of this grace.

Looking back at the ministry to the Ninevites, Jonah came preaching, "Yet forty days, and Nineveh shall be overthrown" (Jonah 3:4). Jonah then informs the reader, "The people of Nineveh believed God" (Jonah 3:5). In Ninevah's case, the threat of God's wrath is met with repentance. Notice,

> The word reached the king of Nineveh, and he arose from his throne, removed his robe, covered himself with sackcloth, and sat in ashes. And he issued a proclamation and published through Nineveh, "By the decree of the king and his nobles: Let neither man nor beast, herd nor flock, taste anything. Let them not feed or drink water, but let man and beast be covered with sackcloth, and let them call out mightily to God. Let everyone turn from his evil way and from the violence that is in his hands. Who knows? God may turn and relent and turn from his fierce anger, so that we may not perish." When God saw what they did, how they turned from their evil way, God relented of the disaster that he had said he would do to them, and he did not do it. (Jonah 3:6–10)

Jonah's account is an excellent example of biblical repentance. The threat of God's wrath requires man "to turn from his evil way."

Man, for his part, attempts to convince God of the seriousness of his decision to turn away from his rebellion by demonstrating physical, mental, spiritual, and psychological suffering. For the king and the citizens of Nineveh, "repentance" did not involve coming to faith in God in the New Testament sense. It involved a change in their behavior to turn away his wrath. For the people of Nineveh, repentance was not coming to faith in Jesus but a decision to heed God's warning. Robert N. Wilkin's summary is essentially correct when he states,

> The repentance of the Ninevites was not faith in Christ and it was not a necessary precursor to faith in Christ. They decided to turn from their sins because they hoped to escape the destruction of their city and the widespread loss of lives that Jonah had proclaimed ("Who can tell if God will turn and relent, and turn away His fierce anger, so that we may not perish?"—Jonah 3:9)

The call to repent is not always a step to gain eternal life or synonymous with "coming to faith" and should not require proof beyond the context of the passage: "When God saw what they did . . . they turned from their evil way." The people in Ninevah changed their behavior to turn away God's wrath.

The Central Message of John the Baptist

If, as we suggest, the good news from God highlights the coming physical manifestation of God's wrath on earth, which foreshadows judgment of the wicked, then there is no surprise that the message of John the Baptist warned of God's impending judgment. John used two metaphors of judgment in his message, which are recorded in Matthew and Luke. Both project a harvest separation with a fiery destiny for those who fail to repent. The first metaphor involves the tree fallen by an axe. John declares, "Even now, the axe is laid on the root of the trees. Every tree, therefore, that does not bear good fruit is cut down and thrown into the fire" (Matt. 3:10–12).

The second metaphor of judgment involves the wheat harvest, symbolized by the winnowing fork. John states,

> "His winnowing fork is in his hand, and he will clear his threshing floor and gather his wheat into the barn, but the chaff he will burn with unquenchable fire." (Matt. 3:12)

With this final metaphor, Matthew ends his account of the ministry and message of John the Baptist. Thus, having begun with a summary of John's message, "Repent, for the kingdom of heaven is at hand," we see the defining traits of John's entire message. Notice: (1) The judgment is imminent. (2) The separation of peoples is near at hand. (3) The repentant will enter the Messiah's kingdom. (4) The unrepentant will be burned "with unquenchable fire."

Only by aligning one's behavior with God's commands can anyone hope to escape his coming judgment. Luke adds another note of importance relative to John's ministry. He states, "So with many other exhortations, he [John] preached good news to the people."

In Luke 4:43, 8:1, and 16:16, "the kingdom of God" defines the good news. Essentially, John the Baptist preached the good news of the kingdom, which Jesus also preached (Matt. 4:23).

The Gospel of John focuses very narrowly on John the Baptist's ministry and message. All four Gospel accounts refer to his prophetic announcement, "After me comes he who is mightier than I, the strap of whose sandal I am not worthy to untie. I have baptized you with water, but he will baptize you with the Holy Spirit."

The Gospel of John is unique from the other Gospels in that the writer records John the Baptist explicitly identifying the Lord Jesus as the Lamb of God who takes away the sin of the world (1:29) and as "the Son of God" (1:34). Many conclude based on John 1:36 that the apostle John is one of the disciples of John the Baptist who became a disciple of the Lord Jesus.

The Gospel of John focuses on only two events in the life of John the Baptist. The writer focuses on John the Baptist's Spirit-inspired prophetic utterances. None of the Gospel accounts indicates how long John's ministry lasted or how long he was in prison. However, John's certainty about Jesus' identity dwindled after his imprisonment by Herod. Matthew 11 reports that he sent two of his disciples to question Jesus, "Are you the one who is to come, or shall we look for another?"

The Importance of Galilee

A second critically important point about the beginning of our Lord's ministry and message is that Jesus began his public ministry in Galilee. Mark 1:9 affirms, "In those days Jesus came from Nazareth of Galilee and was baptized by John in the Jordan." John's call was to righteous living so one would be worthy of God's coming kingdom. Thus, Jesus would need to do the same thing every other man would: live a holy life.

After his baptism by John, the Lord's three temptations by Satan occurred in the wilderness. After this, the Lord returned to Bethany, after which he journeyed to Capernaum (John 2:12). Jesus attended Passover in Jerusalem, then spent time baptizing with some of his disciples in the Judean countryside (John 3:22). Report of his ministry (John 4:1–3) caused the Lord to move back to Galilee. At this point, we pick up the story in Mark's account.

As Jesus returned to Galilee and headed to his home in Nazareth, he began his proclamation. (One would think that Jesus would have begun his public ministry in Jerusalem. Yet, it is Galilee of the Gentiles that had this honor. Jerusalem will play the central role at the end of the Lord's ministry.) Thus, as Jesus began his ministry, he called for repentance in response to his announcement of "the good news of the sovereign administration of God" (Mark 1:14–15). The third chapter of the Gospel of John records that "Jesus and his disciples went into the Judean countryside, and he remained there with them and was baptizing." Later in chapter four, John clarifies that "Jesus himself did not baptize, but only his disciples."

There is no explicit basis to claim that the disciples of Jesus were baptizing people into Christ in a salvational sense. The Pharisees do not seem to associate our Lord's baptism with the baptism of John. Instead, the issue appears to be the relative merits of John's baptism because Jesus surpasses John in the number of individuals submitting to his baptism. John explains to his disciples that because of who Jesus is, it is only natural that he should see more success. John clarifies at the beginning of chapter four that once Jesus learned that the Pharisees heard that he was "making and baptizing more disciples than John...he left Judea and departed again for Galilee."

That Jesus would stop baptizing and return to Galilee ought to make plain that his baptism had no salvational significance. In fact, John the Baptist is recorded as saying, "Whoever believes in the Son has eternal life" (John 3:36). The opposite is also true. No Son, no life. Such a one will experience the wrath of God. That the only use of the term "wrath" in John's Gospel falls from the lips of John the Baptist signals that "the good news of the kingdom" is his focus. One is under God's wrath now. Repentance removes it.

In light of the good news of the sovereign administration of God, repentance should be every man's priority. The urgency of repentance is directly tied to one's belief about our Lord's proclamation. Thus, the Lord calls for "repentance and belief in the good news."

Contextually, Jesus did not refer to his death, burial, and resurrection as "the gospel" or the correct translation "the good news" anywhere in Matthew, Mark, Luke, or John's Gospels. The closest reference to Mark 1:15 of good news" is Mark 1:14—the good news from God concerning the royal rule.

The good news from God is not the good news of Christ's death, burial, and resurrection for the forgiveness of sins. In Mark 1:15, the call to believe in the good news of God by our Lord is a call to prepare to live under the physical manifestation of God's sovereign administration on earth. In the ministry and message of Jesus and his disciples, we see that the rule of heaven has come to earth.

It is a good hermeneutical principle to define terms, ideas, or concepts by the reference closest to the term, idea, or concept in question. In this case, the good news of Mark 1:15 finds a definition in Mark 1:14's "the good news of God."

CHAPTER 7

The Parable of the Soils

Mark 1:14–15

Now after John [the Baptist] had been handed over to the prison, Jesus came into Galilee, shouting out loud the good news from God consisting of "The time is fulfilled, and the sovereign administration of God is at hand; repent and believe in the good news [from God]." (author's translation)

Mark 1:14–15 is the key to understanding the Gospel of Mark. G.R. Beasley-Murray is not the only scholar of reputation who has captured the significance of this passage. His summary reflects precisely what we believe:

This passage, set by Mark as the climax to his prologue to the ministry of Jesus . . . is intended to supply a summary of the gospel preached by Jesus, of which the teaching of Jesus in the body of the gospel can be viewed as exposition.[72]

Sadly, though Mark tells the reader precisely the essence of our Lord's message, many New Testament students ignore Mark's explicit claim and conclude that the Lord's pre-Easter message is the same as the church's post-Easter message. This conclusion ensures faulty interpretations of our Lord's mission, message, and ministry. One such area that suffers abuse as a result is his kingdom parables.

Many of the kingdom parables are explicitly identified as presenting some aspect of the kingdom of God (Hence why they are called "kingdom parables.") A key to interpreting this parable (and all parables) is that their meaning is not universal. The meaning of a parable is defined by the intent of the person giving it. In the Synoptics, the speaker is the Lord Jesus. If the mission, message, and ministry of Jesus are framed up in Mark 1:14–15, then the focus of his ministry—and, by extension, his parables—is that the long-promised physical manifestation of God's rule on earth has come. This is the "good news from God."

Jude reminds us that this "good news" looks back to Enoch. But in Enoch, the focus doesn't seem like such good news from a human perspective. Notice:

> Enoch, who lived in the seventh generation after Adam, prophesied about these people. He said, "Listen! The Lord is coming with countless thousands of his holy ones to execute judgment on the people of the world. He will convict every person of all the ungodly things they have done and for all the insults that ungodly sinners have spoken against him." (Jude 14–15, NLT).

This passage emphasizes man's judgment because of his behavior. The wrath of God will come physically to earth, evidenced by the judgment of the living. Enoch's message is also the core of John the Baptist, the Lord Jesus, his apostles, and our generation.

The Jews had been waiting for this judgment, but they expected it to fall on their enemies—the Romans. They expected the "good news from God" to manifest itself in the coming of Messiah, who would throw off the yoke of Rome. This expectation existed even in the apostles' minds, who, even after Jesus' resurrection, asked, "Lord, are you at this time going to restore the kingdom to Israel?" (Acts 1:6).

A Journey Too Far

Thus, in announcing "the good news from God," Jesus had a lot of misconceptions to correct. As he begins to unfold the broad mysteries of God's plan, we finally start to understand what God has been planning and executing from the fall of creation. As the Son of God, Jesus Christ fulfilled the promise of the physical manifestation of God on earth—Jesus was God. He faithfully accomplished all that the Father assigned him to do; in return, his reward is to reign over all the world for one thousand years (Revelation 20, Heb. 12:2).

However, not all of the details of God's plan are revealed in the Old Testament. Among them is how long the preparation stage for the kingdom would take. That this restoration would not occur immediately with the revelation of the Messiah was not something that the Jews were expecting.

They turned on him when the Messiah's coming did not happen as they expected. If Jesus did not overthrow the yoke of Rome as they expected the Messiah to do, then in their minds, he must not be the Messiah at all. (See Luke 24:13–21 for this perspective.)

This was not the only aspect of the coming of the "good news from God" that made its message difficult for them to hear. Another aspect was that the Messiah would come in the form of a God-Man—one hundred percent God and one hundred percent man, inseparably united yet without mixture. Today, this concept is accepted by many Christians, but it was not so in Jesus' day. What many now take for granted, the Jews of Jesus' day struggled with immensely.[73]

For many Jews living two thousand years ago, the idea that God would become a man by being born of a woman was beyond fantastic. Remember, every good Jewish person was taught from early childhood to recite the Shema twice daily: "Hear O Israel, the Lord is our God, the Lord is One." This saying—etched into the heart and soul of the Jewish people—affirms Judaism and declares the monotheistic unified wholeness of God. Israel had one God! That he existed as three distinct persons equal in every way, yet with individual distinctions, was incomprehensible to many Jews. Now add to that the idea that God became or added humanity to the Godhood. Is it any wonder the Jews had great difficulty with Jesus and what he said?

The Jews of Jesus' day had long been awaiting God's earthly reign. For fourteen hundred years, they had been waiting and formulating expectations about what this kingdom would look like. Thus, a man who spoke and acted differently than anyone had ever seen walked into fourteen hundred years of conditioning. At no time did Jesus have to convince the people of God's existence or his promises to the Jewish people. He would have to convince the multitudes that he was not only the Messiah but also a Messiah as they had never seen nor conceived—fully God and fully man. Also problematic for the Jews to comprehend was that with the revelation of the God-Man, the mysteries of God's plan would now be open to *all* men and women of faith, Jew and Gentile. For many Jews, it would be a journey too far.

The Hostility of the Crowd Grows

Thus, our Lord's ministry and message had a profound and winnowing impact on those who saw and heard him. One was either moved to belief or hardness of heart. For many religious leaders, it was the latter (Mark 3:5). Mark concludes, "The Pharisees went out and immediately held counsel with the Herodians against him, how to destroy him."

The religious leaders did not merely want to stop Jesus' ministry and message; they aimed to see him dead without any hope of God's redemption. Members of Jesus' family began to say, "He is out of his mind" (Mark 3:21). The religious leaders from Jerusalem ascribed his ministry to Beelzebub (Mark 3:22).

Having already alluded to the size of the crowds pressing against the Lord (Mark 3:9), the fourth chapter of Mark opens with the report that the boat he previously ordered (Mark 3:9) was ready. Not everyone in the crowd was a friend. Our Lord's enemies were growing and looking to trap him with his own words to seize him and put him to death. Thus, two groups were ever-present: insiders and outsiders. Insiders bore no ill will for Jesus. Outsiders did!

Unlike the parable-filled chapter of Matthew 13, which contains eight parables,[74] Mark 4 contains only three explicit parables: (1) the parable of the sower (Mark 4:3–9, 13–20); (2) the parable of the earth bearing fruit by itself (Mark 4:26–29); and (3) the parable of the mustard seed (Mark 4:30–32).[75] Mark limited his utilization of parables to only three, each dealing with seeds, growth, and production. This is a clue about the intent of Mark's account.

To appreciate the fourth chapter of Mark, we need to have a good understanding of what both precedes and follows it. What precedes it is our Lord's appointment of the Twelve "so that they might be with him and he might send them out to preach and have authority to cast out demons" (Mark 3:13–19). What follows is his sending out of the Twelve to do precisely that (Mark 6:7–13). Between the appointment and the sending are instructions. Mark 6:12 shows that their preaching consisted of "the good news of the sovereign administration of God," in light of which men and women should repent and believe the good news. Also, in this "between section" are the parables.

Why are these instructions necessary? Just as with the Lord Jesus, the message and ministry of God's good news will not see national and international success to the degree one might expect. This lack of success is not the fault of the message, ministry, or methods of Jesus or his workers. Instead, Jesus explains that the problem is in the hearers' hearts. The majority will reject the message. The parabolic section of Mark 4:1–34 explains why this is the case.

If one completely removes from one's thinking the good news about Jesus Christ (the death, burial, and resurrection of Jesus for the forgiveness of sins), then the correct interpretation of Mark 4 is possible. Nowhere is this more essential than in the interpretation of the kingdom parables. The gospel of Christ is not the focus nor goal of Jesus' teaching in Mark 4; rather, it is the gospel of God.

Having set the stage by explaining the constituent groups among the crowds pressing against the Lord, Mark 4 describes Jesus' attempt to physically and spiritually separate himself from the masses. Thus, Jesus divides the people into two groups: insiders and outsiders. Mark 4:1–2 begins,

> Again, he [Jesus] started to teach along the seashore. For a very large crowd gathered before him so much so that he had to step onto a boat and set himself on the sea as the whole crowd faced him from the shore. Now he began ongoing instructions to them by means of parables. (author's translation).

If we follow A.T. Robertson's chronology of the Gospels, the events detailed in Mark 4 occur at most 18 months before Jesus' crucifixion.[76] Perhaps this gives more insight into why he needed to continue his ministry in stealth. Our Lord will need to teach his disciples much more, but he will also need to limit his critics' cases against him by limiting the understood truths he speaks in their presence. Their case will be built with false accusations at his eventual trial because he gave them so little truth they could understand.

For the first time, Mark informs his readers that Jesus began his stealth campaign by masking truths of the kingdom with simple stories. Mark does not begin with a definition or explanation of what a parable is or does. Rather, he gives an example first.

Mark 4:2b–9

Now in his teaching, he said to them: "Listen! Behold, a sower went out to sow. And as he sowed, a seed fell along the path, and the birds came and devoured it. Another seed fell on rocky ground, where it did not have much soil, and immediately it sprang up since it had no depth of soil. And when the sun rose, it was scorched, and since it had no root, it withered away. Another seed fell among thorns, and the thorns grew up and choked it, and it yielded no grain. And other seeds fell into good soil and it kept producing grain, growing up and increasing and kept yielding thirtyfold and sixtyfold and a hundredfold." And he said, "He who has ears to hear, let him hear." (author's translation)

Since Mark illustrates what a parable is, we should limit our definition to his usage. When evaluating Matthew's account, it is best to see that our Lord gave a series of parables (Matt. 13:3) while on the boat. After he had done so, Mark informs us that "when he [Jesus] was alone, those around him with the twelve kept asking him about the parables." This indicates that the teaching from the boat is over, and the Lord is debriefing the Twelve and other listeners. The imperfect aspect of the verb "to ask" suggests ongoing questioning. This usage supports the idea that the insiders kept asking Jesus about each parable given during his sea-based teaching.

Mark indicates that the disciples (the Twelve and others = insiders) asked the Lord about the parables. Were they asking, "Why do you speak in parables?" or were they asking, "What is the meaning of each parable?" Matthew 13:10 indicates that they were concerned with *why* he was speaking parables. Even though Mark and Luke focus on the meaning of the parables, do not miss this point: neither the insiders nor the outsiders understood the point Jesus was making. The key difference is who requested more information.

Our Lord's answer in Mark 4:11 focuses on both usage and meaning. He states, "To you all [those around him with the Twelve = insiders] has been given [to know] the secret of the kingdom of God, but for those outside, everything is in parables."

Thus, the purpose of the parables is to tell stories everyone can hear (both insiders and outsiders) but to limit the real message to those who want to know more (insiders). The audience on this occasion included "those around him with the Twelve." Concerning this larger group, it is vital that we not divide them into saved and lost or disciple and non-disciple. Remember that, at this point, Judas is one of the Twelve.[77] Also, disciples make decisions daily regarding their commitment to abide with Christ or to leave him (John 6:64, 66). These are not decisions regarding salvation in our modern sense. Some come to Jesus, hear, and stay. These Jesus labels as "true disciples" (John 8:31). Others come, hear, and wait awhile. Lastly, some come, hear, and immediately leave—remember the four soils.

To assume all are saved or lost is to miss the point. It would have been challenging to find a Jewish person living during the ministry of Jesus who did not believe in the God of Abraham, Isaac, and Jacob or was not waiting for God's long-promised deliverer. They believed in God's promises to these men, which became the basis of their lives, daily religious practice, and future expectations. One of those expectations was that God was going to act on those promises very soon and that this would ultimately result in the removal of Roman slavery. This faith (in the promises of God) is the essence of Abraham's journey to righteousness, as reflected in Genesis 15:6.

The issue for many Jews was figuring out how Jesus fit into God's plans. As Jesus revealed that all the promises recorded in the Law, the Prophets, and the Writings found fulfillment in him, many could not comprehend it. Modern readers take for granted many of the concepts and ideas Jesus preached two thousand years ago. However, in the first century, Jesus was a radical by any measure. Thus, a Jew could have believed in the promises of God and received God's righteousness and still not have believed in Jesus.

Our point here is that whatever the distinction between the inside and those on the outside, it is not an issue of saved and lost. It also is noteworthy that once Jesus explained the facts to the insiders, they could have explained them to the outsiders.

The last point that should inform our understanding of the outsiders' identity compared to the insiders is that the insiders did not understand the meaning of the parables either.

Were it not for Jesus' explanation, they would have remained just as ignorant as the outsiders of God's sovereign administration!

Our Lord is not involved in a bait and switch. His stories communicate real, permanent truth for those who draw near to him for understanding. What does he intend by the phrase "the secret of the kingdom of God?" Unlike both Matthew and Luke, Mark does not include the infinitive form of the verb "to know; understand." It is our conviction that the infinitive is understood—that it must be supplied as it appears in the accounts of both writers.

Given that the insiders were no more able than the outsiders to "get" the meaning of the parables without our Lord's enlightenment, additional knowledge is the big difference between the two groups. Most modern translations render the Greek *mystērion* as "secret" (singular) in Mark 4:11. The reason is well reflected in the comments of France when he writes:

> *The mention of a μυστήριον immediately sets the tone for Jesus' response, but can easily mislead English readers who naturally think of a 'mystery' as something which is inherently hard to understand, and which can be unravelled only by unusual cleverness—if it is not totally incomprehensible. But the true sense of μυστήριον is better captured by the English 'secret', which denotes not incomprehensibility but hiddenness. A secret is that which is not divulged—but once known it need not be hard to grasp. It is privileged information rather than a puzzle.*[78]

Thus, the parables of our Lord allowed information to be shared in an open area without divulging the "secret meaning" that only the speaker knew. While Matthew and Luke make clear by their use of secrets (plural), Mark is concerned with one secret: the sovereign administration of God. We believe that by "secret" (singular), Mark refers to the fundamental core value upon which all other insights about the kingdom are based. Indeed, for Mark, the parable of the sower (Matt. 13:18) is "the parable about parables."[79]

Why Keep It a Secret?

In chapter three of this book, we defined the phrase "the kingdom of God." We concluded that "the sovereign administration of God" better reflects the intended textual meaning. The physical manifestation of God's rule has come to earth. Contrary to the belief of many of the Jews at the time, the presence of God physically on earth would not result in an immediate challenge to the political establishment. The secret of the sovereign administration of God explains why.

Given the self-evident capabilities of Jesus to set aside natural law, control entirely the kingdom of darkness, and heal every kind of disease, confusion reigned among the Jews. Many were asking why Jesus would not "just do it"! The reason is the secret of the sovereign administration. However, this information is withheld from those who are outside: "To you has been given the secret of the kingdom of God, but for those outside, everything comes in parables: so that they may indeed look, but not perceive, and may indeed listen, but not understand" (Mark 4:11). There is much debate among scholars regarding what two groups are represented in this verse. "To you" refers to "those around him with the Twelve." "Those outside" must be defined contextually.

Because of their disgust with Jesus, Mark 3:6 reports that "the Pharisees went out and immediately held counsel with the Herodians against him, how to destroy him." The Pharisees went out from our Lord's presence, displaying their unbelief (hardness of heart). Mark 3:13 highlights that Jesus "called to him those whom he desired." There is debate about the actual number of individuals called. Whether he called just twelve men or a larger group from which he chose the Twelve is not clear. However, our emphasis is on the call itself. Unlike the hard-hearted Pharisees who went out of his presence, his disciples entered his presence—they sought it.

Mark 3:21 indicates that personal family members "went out to seize him, for they were saying, 'He is out of his mind.'" Mark 3:31 also places family members "outside." Again, we see those who do not believe our Lord's report as being outside. The third chapter of Mark ends with our Lord declaring that "whoever does the will of God, he is my brother and sister and mother."

The ultimate example of obedience is believing that God sent Jesus. Therefore, we see a clear delineation between "those outside" who do not do the will of God and "those inside" who do.

Jesus began his ministry by calling "to repent and believe in the good news." Those who desire to come and remain in the Lord's presence receive the secrets of the sovereign administration of God. Both insiders and outsiders hear parables, but unlike those who are privy to the Lord's decoding (private interpretation), the outsiders remain unilluminated.

Mark 4:12 explains why this is the case. The meaning of Mark 4:12 has found little consensus among Scripture students regarding the text's intent. The text says, "So that 'they may indeed see but not perceive, and may indeed hear but not understand, lest they should turn and be forgiven.'"

The use of parables keeps outsiders ignorant because, as we will discuss, only the speaker of the parables knows its intent. Since outsiders refuse to come into Jesus' presence, they are locked from understanding. Jesus states that the price of unbelief in the good news from God is continued ignorance of the opportunity to join the ruling class of his coming kingdom on earth, which has begun.

Isaiah 6:9–10, which our Lord quotes, is among the most debated Old Testament passages used in the Gospels. France gives an excellent summary of the reason for so much debate. Please notice as he writes so eloquently:

> *The content of these verses is apparently quite simple: a limited group, apart from the crowd, ask Jesus about parables, and he explains that while they are privileged to understand the secret of the kingdom of God, others have everything in parables, in*

order that they will not share that saving understanding. But few [scholars] have been content to believe that Jesus really meant to say just that, and there are sufficient ambiguities or obscurities in the wording to allow wide scope for scholarly ingenuity to discover a more acceptable intent.... In particular the condensed quotation of Is. 6:9–10 in v. 12 provides ample room for debate, both as to the original sense of the Isaiah prophecy and as to the significance of its application to Jesus' parables.[80]

We agree with France that "the content of these verses is quite simple." We agree that "sufficient ambiguities or obscurities in the wording...allow wide scope for scholarly ingenuity to discover a more acceptable intent."

However, we disagree that "the outsiders" are denied "saving understanding." Isaiah 6:9–10 is not about being saved or lost. It is about being faithful or unfaithful.

What "the outsiders" are being excluded from is not personal salvation. The overwhelming majority of New Testament scholars share this assumption. The assumption that a "saving understanding" (how one is to be saved) is kept from the "outsiders" offends many and leads them to work overtime to make Mark 4:12 conform to their theological persuasion. Notice Douglas S. McComiskey's comment:

Jesus' quotation of Isa 6:9–10 in the purpose of parables passages raises the question of whether he desired some people not to be saved, which is really the central exegetical issue.[81]

McComiskey and so many others allow this false assumption to control their exegesis. This guarantees an incorrect interpretation every time. The good news of Christ is not in focus. Rather, the controlling theme of our Lord's ministry is the good news from God. This promise was made to mankind as far back as Enoch: God would physically manifest his presence on earth to rule. The secret of the sovereign administration of God is that the God-Man rule extends to men and women. There is not going to be a single King, but many kings (Matt. 19:28, Rev. 3:21). The ultimate opportunity of inclusion in kingdom leadership is earned by faith works. Sadly, few will have sufficient fruit to earn commendation, exaltation, and honoration. This is what we shall discover when our Lord interprets this parable.

What Does It Mean to "Be Saved"?

Isaiah 6:9–10 falls within one of the greatest (if not the greatest) chapters in the book's first half. The call of Isaiah to deliver a prophetic word occurs in the context of one of the most remarkable manifestations of God's physical presence on earth before the incarnation of Christ recorded in Scripture. Isaiah 6 does not describe the conversion of Isaiah in a New Testament sense. To believe that Isaiah "got saved" in chapter six is to misunderstand salvation in the Old Testament entirely.

Just as with Abraham, salvation came to a man or woman by faith in God's promise(s). Isaiah's message to Judah is not a call to faith. It is a call to faithfulness/faithful sonship.

Isaiah 6 shows that when a person who believes in God's existence and holds to his promises is privileged to personally see the physical manifestation of God on earth (the good news from God), man's first response should be humility. It is unclear whether the theophanic manifestation is of God the Father or a pre-incarnate appearance of the Lord Jesus. Still, it does not matter because the point is God's physical manifestation on earth. Sadly, it would not be permanent. However, in Jesus, the first step to permanency occurred.

With the "otherness" of God and man's "unlikeness of God" firmly established in the mind of Isaiah, i.e., God is not like us, and we are not like God, Isaiah becomes an instrument of use for God's glory. Isaiah is on a roll with such a glorious manifestation of God, the true anointing, and a call to deliver a message from God to Judah. However, once Isaiah receives the deliverable, optimism turns to pessimism. The long-promised exile for disobedience has been set in motion. His message will confirm that repentance that turns away wrath is no longer possible—not because God no longer desires it, but because man's heart is beyond repentance. God commands Isaiah to state the facts of the peoples' prolonged history of willful rebellion against his commands. Instead of producing repentance, Isaiah's message will produce the opposite effect—hardheartedness.

God declares,

> "Go, and say to this people: 'Keep on hearing, but do not understand; keep on seeing, but do not perceive.' Make the heart of this people dull, and their ears heavy, and blind their eyes; lest they see with their eyes, and hear with their ears, and understand with their hearts, and turn and be healed." (Isa. 6:9–10)

"Keep on hearing, but do not understand; keep on seeing, but do not perceive" perfectly describes the conduct of Judah for 490 years. By this time, possibly as many as four prophets had called the people to live in righteousness consistently, but the people's seesaw relationship had degenerated into continual evil.

Unlike the prophets of the past who called Judah to repentance to avert exile, Isaiah tells the people that that exile is now inescapable. By telling Judah the truth, Isaiah will only cause her to hasten her destiny. More than one prophet was killed for telling the people the truth. Isaiah 6:9–10 describes the cause-effect behavior that occurs repeatedly throughout Judah's history. A NT parallel occurs in the book of

Acts. When confronted with the truth, the Jews responded to Stephen exactly as Isaiah described. Stephen declared, "You stiff-necked people, uncircumcised in heart and ears, you always resist the Holy Spirit. As your fathers did, so do you." (Acts 7:51)

Notice the Jews' reaction,

Now when they heard these things they were enraged, and they ground their teeth at him...they cried out with a loud voice and stopped their ears and rushed together at him. (Acts 7:54–55, 57).

"Make the heart of this people dull, and their ears heavy, and blind their eyes" describes the effect the truth will have on the people. The clause "lest they see with their eyes, and hear with their ears, and understand with their hearts, and turn and be healed" does not mean that God is responsible for the people's failure to repent.

For 490 years, God sought repentance. Dead prophets and written threats prove it. God describes to Isaiah the impact of telling Judah the truth. Just as the Jews responded to Stephen, Judah responded to Isaiah. God responds to their behavior.

Our Lord's use of Isaiah 6:9–10 in Mark 4:11–12 has an opposite intent. Unlike Isaiah, who told the people the truth only to see them act as the Jews did with Stephen—rush to destruction—our Lord hides the truth to prevent the rejectors (the outsiders) from any possibility of "entering the kingdom of God."

Thus, I would rewrite France's otherwise excellent comment to say,

The content of Mark 4:11–12 is apparently quite simple: a limited group, apart from the crowd, ask Jesus about parables, and he explains that while they are privileged to understand the secret of the kingdom of God, others have everything in parables in order that they will not share in the sovereign administration of God.

Why would the King allow rejectors of his right to rule to serve in his elite administration? Such behavior might be humanistic, but it has no place in the divine workings of God's coming rule on earth. This is the very point of the parable of the sower.

Having defined the difference between insiders and outsiders, the Lord will now explain "the secret of the sovereign administration of God" to the insiders. In essence, who and how one earns the right to reign with Christ is opposite from the national expectations of the Jews. Kingdom inclusion and leadership participation are not hereditary. Nor is it limited to Jews only. It must be earned. By "right to reign," we mean to participate in the administration of the day-to-day affairs of state once the "not yet" aspect of our Lord's rule begins.

Mark 4:13–20 returns to the parable of the sower with a detailed explanation. While Mark lists three parables, he only records one detailed explanation for one of them. Thus, the parable of the sower is of great importance to Mark's storyline. This section begins with a question our Lord asks the insiders, "Do you all not understand this parable? How then will you understand all the parables?" (Mark 4:13). This, also, indicates the importance of this parable.

Our Lord's first question makes perfect sense here. By definition, a parable's meaning cannot be discerned by the hearer unless the author explains his intent. What a parable represents or is intended to mean is known only in the speaker's mind. A parable without authorial intent is another typical everyday story of some human action. The parable of the sower has the breadth to represent many truths. Only the author (in this case, Jesus) knows his intent, which he must explain for accurate communication.

The point of our Lord's rhetorical question is to strengthen the insiders' understanding that they will need unique insight that can only come from Jesus. Neither insiders nor outsiders can understand the Lord's parables without his explanation. Thus, it is all the more critical that the insiders stay close to Jesus.

The second question, "How then will you understand all the parables?" signals the importance of the parable of the sower. In this regard, Guelich is very helpful when he states, "The second question, "How will you understand all the parables" ...indicates the significance of this parable for understanding the others".[82]

God has decreed that all insiders will be given the secret of the kingdom of God. This is the essence of this parable. It is at this point in the narrative that fulfillment comes. Once explained, insiders will have the necessary components to decipher all the kingdom parables.

The Seed's Identity

"The Sower sows the word." (Mark 4:14)

Neither Mark nor any of the other New Testament writers identify the sower. However, we already see in Mark's account that John the Baptist, Jesus, and his disciples communicate "the good news of the sovereign administration of God." Thus, there is little need to identify a single sower explicitly.

However, Matthew, Mark, and Luke offer insight regarding the seed. Mark identifies the seed as "the word" (Mark 4:14). Matthew adds that the seed is "the word about the kingdom" (Matt. 13:19). Finally, Luke adds that the seed is "the word of God" (Luke 8:11). At first glance, it would seem to be an ironclad case for identifying the "seed" as the gospel of Christ, which is precisely what a majority of NT scholars conclude.

The majority of New Testament teachers automatically assume that the seed is the modern Gospel message. They rush head-on to teach that the soils represent various responses to the message of our Lord's death, burial, and resurrection for the forgiveness of sin. **This isn't true**. The complete phrase that most accurately defines the seed is "the word about the sovereign administration of God," which Luke on three separate occasions explicitly identifies as the core message of Jesus Christ (Luke 4:43, 8:1, 16:16). As Jesus went about preaching throughout the land of Israel, he proclaimed God's invitation for men to earn a spot in the coming administration of God's rule on earth. How men and women respond to this message is the point of the parable of the sower.

The First Soil's Response

"And these are the ones along the path, where the word is sown: when they hear, Satan immediately comes and takes away the word that is sown in them." (Mark 4:15)

The description of the first response covers the first of three responses of the outsiders who may or may not be believers in our modern sense. Their rejection of the messenger ensures their ignorance of his message. When outsiders hear the message about the sovereign administration of God, they do not understand it, allowing the devil to take the message away easily. Matthew 13:19 describes the problem of hearing with no understanding.

It is critically important to remember that Mark 1:14–15 informs us that Jesus began his public ministry, shouting out loud the good news from God. The good news from God was not given in parabolic form. People heard, saw, and personally experienced evidence of God's physical manifestation on earth for over two years. The secret is not the sovereign administration of God itself. Instead, it is how men will respond to the message about it. The consequences of an incorrect response are not good. Notice how Luke describes it: "The devil comes and takes away the word from their hearts, so that they may not believe and be saved" (Luke 8:12).

Now, most readers will automatically conclude that Luke 8:12 describes people who miss out on salvation. Balz and Schneider identify this clause as purpose,[83] which is insignificant given that Boyer identifies "the vast majority" of these clauses as valid purpose clauses (97%)[84] in the New Testament. Thus, the devil's purpose is to take "the word from" the outsider's hearts "so that they may not believe and be saved." Perhaps more than any other detail, Luke's description supports those who see personal salvation as the theological focus here. Clearly, "to not believe and be saved" refers to the rejection of the gospel of Christ in their thinking. However, when this parable was given, there had been no explicit declaration that our Lord's death, burial, and resurrection for the forgiveness of a person's sins had been preached or understood by the disciples or anyone else. The twelve disciples certainly did not see our Lord's death as necessary to save men and women from eternal punishment. Peter's reaction to Jesus' first explicit announcement of his imminent death was met with derision and rebuke. (See Matt 16:21–23.)

Jesus' earliest prediction of his death occurs in a heated exchange between Jesus and the Pharisees regarding a sign to prove his authenticity. Jesus responds to their request by saying,

> "An evil and adulterous generation seeks for a sign, but no sign will be given to it except the sign of the prophet Jonah. For just as Jonah was three days and three nights in the belly of the great fish, so will the Son of Man be three days and three nights in the heart of the earth." (Matt. 12:39–40)

There is no evidence that the Pharisees understood what Jesus meant by this statement, and there is no indication that the disciples understood it. Even if they had, they would not have understood why it would be necessary for Jesus to die. Modern readers mustn't read subsequent theological developments back into what Jesus meant. We know it now, not how the original audience understood it two thousand years ago.

While there are those of certain theological persuasions who might accept the notion that the devil can stop a person from coming to faith in Jesus Christ, we are not among them. Are you among those who believe that the devil can take the Gospel from the heart of unbelievers and thereby keep them from coming to faith in Christ? If Luke 8:12 refers to salvation in the sense of having your sins forgiven by the blood of Jesus Christ through faith, then you are forced to this conclusion.

If the devil could prevent any man from coming to faith in Jesus Christ, why would any man ever come to faith? Why would the devil allow some to hear, understand, and believe in Jesus but not others? If he had the power to stop a person from obtaining salvation, wouldn't he want to stop the salvation of all?

For an accurate interpretation, we must understand Luke 8:12 historically. That is, when Jesus spoke the parable, the gospel of God was the focus, not the gospel of Christ. This passage does not automatically refer to personal, spiritual salvation. Luke 8:50 says, "Do not fear; only believe, and she will be well." The Greek says, "Do not fear; only believe, and she will be saved," which is reflected in the New Revised Standard Version. The context indicates that "to be saved" means to be healed of physical sickness. There is no emphasis on spiritual salvation here.[85]

Likewise, Luke 8:48 is about the woman with the discharge of blood who believed that if she touched Jesus, she would be saved (healed). Jesus tells her, "Daughter, your faith has made you well; go in peace."

In Greek, it says, "Daughter, your faith has saved you." "To be saved" does not automatically refer to spiritual salvation in every case. The devil cannot stop spiritual salvation, but he can stop progressive sanctification. One of his chief means of doing so is ignorance. By stealing the unrecognized truth from the hearts of outsiders, the devil keeps them ignorant of God's will. In this case, they continue to ignore "the good news of the sovereign administration of God." No progress is made in their lives to earn the right to sit with Christ as rulers in the coming kingdom of Christ.

Just as our Lord declared in Mark 1:14–15, the correct response of men and women to the message of God's sovereign administration is to "repent and believe the good news from God." This response delivers them from the coming wrath of God and may, with effort, earn them superior positions of honor in the coming administration of the Lord Jesus Christ.

The Second Soil's Response

"And these are the ones sown on rocky ground: the ones who, when they hear the word [about the sovereign administration of God], immediately receive it with joy. But they have no root in themselves, thus endure for a while; then, when tribulation or persecution arises on account of the word [about the sovereign administration of God], immediately they fall away." (Mark 4:16, author's translation)

The second type of response describes a temporary acceptance until trouble changes their minds. Matthew's description of the second possible response is similar to Mark's. However, Luke adds, "They believe for a while, and in time of testing fall away." Thus, for those who advance the false narrative that spiritual salvation is in focus here, Luke's wording is additional proof for seeing the gospel of Christ in focus rather than the gospel of God. Is it any wonder Arminians feel good about their interpretation? However, only by reading modern conclusions back into the text does one find support for this position.

Believing the good news from God does not necessarily result in spiritual salvation, but this is what some think. One should ask, "What do the hearers believe for a while?" What is the object of their belief? The text says, "The word." What word? The word about God's sovereign administration is: "Repent, for the kingdom of God [heaven], is at hand."

One who hears this message will need personal salvation to comply fully. Personal salvation may be included in the response of a hearer, but in the preaching of John the Baptist, the Lord Jesus, and his disciples, it is not exclusively the desired response as seen.

Failure to recognize this fact causes interpreters to do gymnastics with the text. Notice how the *BKC* handles Luke 8:13:

> The fact that they believe for a while but . . . fall away means that they only accept the facts of the Word mentally and then reject it when "the going gets rough." It does not mean they lose their salvation, for they had none to lose.[86]

The Bible Knowledge Commentary says precisely what we would expect from those who do not see a distinction between the gospel of God and the gospel of Christ. For Calvinists, the lack of distinction is necessary to prevent the Arminian conclusion that loss of salvation is possible. This kind of reasoning drives those who read modern views back into the text. Luke says they "receive [the word about the sovereign administration of God] with joy." Of the 56 times the verb "to take, receive" occurs in the New Testament, there is no single example of a distinction in meaning as *The Bible Knowledge Commentary* advances.

John Nolland gets it half right. He states,

> *Luke changes Mark's verb for "they receive" to δέχονται and thus creates a phrase with the following "the word" which elsewhere regularly indicates a believing response to the preaching of the gospel (Acts 8:14; 11:1; 17:11; 1 Thess. 1:6; 2:13; Jas. 1:21).*

Every word in Nolland's statement is correct. However, he fails to distinguish between the Lord Jesus's pre-Easter message and the Apostles' post-Easter message. There is no evidence of a half-hearted mental game being played here. True belief in the gospel of God occurs and should be understood by the interpreter.

Temporary belief in the good news from God is possible. The good news that God has opened up the candidacies for rulers in the leadership of his coming kingdom creates joy in the hearts of our Lord's disciples. Excitement about the offer fades when the reality of the price required becomes clearly understood. "When tribulation or persecution arises because of the word [about the sovereign administration of God]," the once excited disciples stop following Jesus. John 6:60–70 perfectly illustrates this point. The most challenging question is why this word brings such tribulation or persecution. So, we ask, "Who sponsors the "time of testing?" Who ensures that "tribulation or persecution arises on account of the word" in the lives of the second soil?

Scripture confirms on more than one occasion that "troubles" will come to those who commit to living under God's rule (Mark 8:35; 10:29–30; John 16:33; Acts 14:22). Again, we ask, "Why?"

Challenging the God of This World

The word about the sovereign administration of God directly challenges the authority of Satan, the god of this world. The message of God's rule from heaven coming to earth is met with resistance, with Satan evidencing his displeasure through those whom he can influence. All three accounts of the parable of the sower explicitly identify God's arch-enemy (Mark: "Satan"; Matthew: "the evil one"; Luke: "the devil") at work against God's plan. While explicit identification is made regarding the evil one's involvement in the adverse outcomes of the first soil, the lack of such an overt identification in the remaining soils should not be taken to mean that he isn't trying.

What Luke calls a "time of testing" (Luke 8:13), both Matthew and Mark call "tribulation or persecution because of the word." The noun *peirasmos* occurs a total of twenty-one times in the New Testament, with six of them occurring in Luke's Gospel. As Louw and Nida make clear, *it* has both a positive and negative nuance. They highlight the positive sense to mean, "To try to learn the nature or character of someone or something by submitting such to thorough and extensive testing."[87] They also indicate a negative sense, "To endeavor or attempt to cause someone to sin— "to tempt, to trap, to lead into temptation."[88]

Thus, we advance the notion that God tests his people, but Satan tempts them. God allows and encourages such testing. The first occurrence of this noun in the Gospel of Luke concerns Jesus being "led by the Spirit in the wilderness for forty days, being tempted by the devil" (Luke 4:1). After three separate unsuccessful attempts, Luke reports that "when the devil had ended every temptation, he departed from him until an opportune time" (Luke 4:13). Notice the connection between "testing" and "time" on both occasions.

Many scholars recognize that the Lord's "time of testing" accounts in Matthew and Luke have close parallels and explicit framing with Deuteronomy 6–8, where Israel's "time of testing" is directly referenced.[89] Deuteronomy 8:2 explicitly states,

> And you shall remember the whole way that the LORD your God has led you these forty years in the wilderness, that he might humble you, *testing* you to know what was in your heart, whether you would keep his commandments or not. (emphasis added)

The expressed purpose of God's tests of Israel was to know what was in her heart and whether she would keep his commandments or not. Compared to Israel, the Lord Jesus is led by the Holy Spirit to be tested by Satan. Jesus is put to three specific temptations: (1) self-sufficiency, (2) self-preservation, and (3) self-exaltation.[90] Unlike unfaithful Israel, the Son of God proved faithful to God's will in that he was willing to wholly depend on God, i.e., being sustained in life and submitting to death when necessary.

Neither the test of Israel nor the Lord Jesus—involved a call to personal salvation. Neither required putting faith in God. Instead, each required being faithful to God in light of his promises.

The second seed responds positively to the sower. A positive response about the word of the kingdom is dampened by a "time of testing," which causes some disciples to "fall away." There is a consensus belief among many New Testament scholars that "to fall away," whether pre-resurrection or post-resurrection,

> refers to the offense that results in the loss of salvation. Depending on whether or not a person already believes, it refers either to a falling away from or a rejection of faith.[91]

The majority opinions take either one of two positions: that personal salvation is lost (Arminian view) or the person was never "truly" saved (Calvinist view). However, there is no explicit declaration in Scripture that a person who falls away forfeits personal salvation. While the Scriptures speak of consequences for those who "fall away," nowhere in Scripture is the eternal lake of fire spoken of as one of them.

In Mark 14:27 (cf. Matt. 26:31), the Lord Jesus explicitly declares, "You will all fall away, for it is written, 'I will strike the shepherd, and the sheep will be scattered.'" All twelve disciples vehemently deny that this will occur (which is further described as denying the Lord). Yet soon enough, our Lord's prediction comes true. Mark 14:66–72 describes Peter's slow descent into apostasy, which concludes with the sad declaration, "He broke down and wept." All too often, modern definitions are forced back on the New Testament text without a good appreciation of the historical circumstances of the text. There is no evidence that Peter and his fellow contemporaries denied the deity of Christ. There is no evidence that they denied the existence of God or his promises. Because one proves to be a coward in the face of tribulation or persecution does not *un-save* a person.

To stumble at a tenet of the Christian faith or the fact that many Jews had a real problem with understanding how Jesus could be the Son of God did not nullify their belief in the God of Abraham, Isaac, and Jacob and/or the promises he made and that formed the basis of their daily expectation of seeing fulfillment.

Two thousand years have passed, and many New Testament saints still do not understand the nature of salvation, primarily because they do not understand the difference between the gospel *from* God and the gospel *about* Jesus Christ.

Many, many disciples refuse to be progressively sanctified. Some refuse out of ignorance, some refuse due to misinformation (false teachings), others refuse out of fear of criticism, and still others refuse due to laziness. None of these conditions causes the loss of salvation. Rewards, on the other hand, are another matter altogether, as we will show later.

The Third Soil's Identity

"And others are the ones sown among thorns. They are those who hear the word, but the cares of the world and the deceitfulness of riches, and the desires for other things enter in and choke the word, and it proves unfruitful." (Mark 4:18–19)

The third type of response to the message of the sovereign administration of God is no different than the first and second in terms of the consequences. The difference is what causes a lack of production. When the word about the sovereign administration of God goes forth, disciples who follow Christ for different reasons are confronted with a choice. The offer to earn elite status in the coming rule of God on earth requires a level of devotion and commitment unparalleled in God's economy. To earn God's favor sufficient to be rewarded with the highest positions of honor in the coming rule of God on earth requires the abandonment of self-sufficiency, self-preservation, and self-exaltation. The longer one listens to Christ, the more one understands the nature of the call and the challenges to faithfulness.

In the third soil, the word (of the sovereign administration of God) becomes unfruitful because it is choked out by "the cares of this world." The only close parallel to the phrase "the cares of the world" occurs in Luke 21:34: "cares of this life." The Greek noun, according to Balz and Schneider, "refers to that which is existentially important, that which monopolizes the heart's concerns."[92] Matthew 6:25 defines the "cares of this life" as follows, "Therefore I tell you, do not be anxious about your life, what you will eat or what you will drink, nor about your body, what you will put on."

The problem described here is a believer who is overly concerned with these concerns to the point that they monopolize every waking moment, and that the person no longer prioritizes earning elite status in God's coming rule. You have to make a choice: God or money!

The second obstacle to obtaining elite status in the coming rule of God on earth is "the deceitfulness of riches." The deceit of wealth is particularly dangerous because of the power of wealth's control over human nature (Matt. 19:23–24)—acquisition and control of wealth blind a person to God's priorities.

By "the desire for other things enter in," Mark makes room for the many other objections of the human heart that take priority over undiluted devotion to obtaining elite status in the coming rule of God. These three influences "choke the word." The word about the sovereign administration of God should move men and women to repentance and faith in the good news from God. Instead, the gatekeepers of men's hearts (i.e., the worries of life, the acquisition of wealth, and worldly desires) prevent men's hearts from the whole "followship" of Christ—the result: unfruitfulness, i.e., no reward in heaven.

The offer of the opportunity to earn elite status in the coming rule of God will prove unmotivating for many followers of Jesus Christ. Once personal salvation is obtained many will not advance in discipleship. Thus, what is absent in the first three soils is fruitfulness. The reason each soil failed to produce fruit is different. However, the outcome is the same: none of the first three soils produced sustainable fruit.

The Fourth Soil's Identity

"But those that were sown on the good soil are the ones who hear the word and accept it and bear fruit, thirtyfold and sixtyfold and a hundredfold." (Mark 4:20)

The last category of disciples is those whose reaction to hearing the word about God's sovereign administration causes them to pursue God's great honor with energy and effort. These are said to be "good soil." They are good in the sense that they produce fruit. There is no inherent goodness. Hearing and accepting the word about God's sovereign administration and bearing fruit evidencing this devotion characterizes "good soil."

All soils heard the word, but three soils accepted it, and only one soil bore fruit. Fruit production is not uniform. Thirty, sixty, and one hundredfold explains why kingdom rewards will differ. The Lord Jesus explains the distribution of rewards in the story of the talents. One, two, and five could become two, four, and ten, with additional rewards as described in the parable.

CHAPTER 8

Other Secrets of the Kingdom

The parable of the sower (Mark 4:1–9) reveals *the* secret of the sovereign administration of God: that elite status in the coming rule of God on earth must be earned by faithful devotion to the commands of God. This status will not come by heredity. Nor will it come based on favoritism. Self-sufficiency, self-preservation, and self-exaltation must be abandoned. Trust in God's sufficiency, preservation, and exaltation will ensure a disciple receives commendation, exaltation, and honoration at the Bema judgment.

Yet many secrets remain about God's sovereign administration. Many of these secrets are revealed in the remainder of Mark 4: Jesus' discussion about the lamp (4:21:15), the parable of the growing seed (4:26:29), and the mustard seed (4:30:32).

Let's start by looking at Jesus' discussion about the lamp.

> And he said to them, "Is a lamp brought in to be put under a basket, or under a bed, and not on a stand? For nothing is hidden except to be made manifest; nor is anything secret except to come to light. If anyone has ears to hear, let him hear." And he said to them, "Pay attention to what you hear: with the measure you use, it will be measured to you, and still more will be added to you. For to the one who has, more will be given, and from the one who has not, even what he has will be taken away." (Mark 4:21–25)

As we read this question, we must consider its context in the more extensive chapter. In this case, it is immediately preceded by the parable of the sower. Thus, the first question is, "Is there a relationship between our Lord's comments about the parable of the sower and the parable of the lamp? If so, what?" Many see our Lord's comments about the lamp (Mark 4:21–23) and his comments about additions and deletions (Mark 4:24–25) as additional parables.[93] Yet it may be better to see them as further insight into the parable of the sower instead.

The content of Mark 4:21–25 appears in several places in Matthew and Luke, as well.[94] Yet, nowhere is this material explicitly identified as a parable. Rather, our Lord's comments appear in his explanation of the parable of the sower. Thus, it is better to see Mark not as recording a new parable but as continuing our Lord's explanation of the significance of the parable of the sower for the insiders.

89

Revelation of Kingdom Rewards

The parable of the sower revealed the secret of the sovereign administration of God. Since leadership status in this administration must be earned, this will necessitate that the identity of the insiders be hidden until the appropriate time. At that time, revelation will come. Our Lord's illustration of this point can be found in Mark 4:21–23. The purpose of bringing a lamp in is not to conceal it (put it under a basket or bed) but to put it on its stand. Like a lamp, it will eventually be exposed even if it is hidden or secret. Insiders will reveal their purpose for all to see. This is part of God's plan.

As with the previous passage, to properly understand Mark 4:24–25, we must place it in its larger context. Here it follows the parable of the talents (Matt. 25:14–30). In this parable, the Lord explained that for faithful disciples, commendation, exaltation, and honoration await. But for unfaithful disciples, there will be denouncement, demotion, and divarication (Matt. 25:26–30). Not only will there be denouncement, demotion, and divarication, but these things will be meted out in proportion to the disciples' actions ("With the measure you use, it will be measured to you," Mark 4:24–25).

In Mark 4:24–25, we learn that insiders and outsiders determine their destinies through actions. Insiders' rewards will be positive, while outsiders' rewards will be negative. Insiders' actions will determine the degree of their gain, while outsiders' actions will determine the degree of their loss.

The Parable of the Growing Seed

Mark 4:26–29 lists the second of three kingdom parables in Mark's account, in which we learn more about the secrets of the administration of the kingdom of God. The parable is unique to Mark's Gospel, but the central message is not. The text reads,

> And he said, "The kingdom of God is as if a man should scatter seed on the ground. He sleeps and rises night and day, and the seed sprouts and grows; he knows not how. The earth produces by itself, first the blade, then the ear, then the full grain in the ear. But when the grain is ripe, at once he puts in the sickle, because the harvest has come."

There is no consensus among scholars concerning how this parable is labeled. Guelich calls it "the parable of the seed's growth."[95] James A. Brooks labels it "the parable of the seed growing spontaneously."[96] Hendriksen and Kistemaker call it the "parable of the seed growing in secret."[97] The title of the parable is ultimately driven by what one sees as its central emphasis. "The sower," "the seed," "secret growth," and "the harvest" are all potential contenders.

Regardless of what we name the parable, the seed motif (which occurs in all three of the explicitly identified parables of Mark 4) appears. The seed is explicitly identified as "the word about the sovereign administration of God, i.e., "Repent, for the kingdom of heaven, is at hand." In the parable of the sower, we discovered who will repent and bring forth fruit worthy of repentance. In this second "seed" parable, we discover that the growth of the royal rule of God will be natural.

In chapter one, Mark introduced the kingdom of God as the central core message of Jesus Christ. Jesus came shouting out loud that the sovereign administration of God on earth had begun. Until Jesus, the physical manifestation of the rule of God had been exercised from heaven through intermediaries (prophets, priests, and kings). With the arrival of the God-Man, that changed. Now, the physical manifestation of the sovereign administration of God—through the Messiah Jesus—began. Throughout Jesus' ministry, we see evidence of this authority as Jesus cast out demons and removed disease, death, and decay.

But for Jesus' listeners, one of the secrets of God's sovereign administration was its development. Jesus' listeners expected God's physical rule on earth to be announced by cataclysmic disturbances in the sky and to result in political upheaval, leading to the people of God ruling from Jerusalem (Zeph. 1:14–18).

However, as we learn from this seed parable, this is not how God's sovereign administration would begin. It would start small without much fanfare, then grow until all of the earth was under its authority. This parable tells us that disciples must not allow the kingdom's slow start to influence their confidence regarding its ultimate manifestation at the King's appearance to rule.

Note that the kingdom's growth is not in the hands of the sower. The initial words of Mark 4:26 should be rendered: "The sovereign administration of God is like a man who scattered the seed on the ground." The introduction draws no particular attention to the sower of the seed. Apart from the scattering and harvesting, the sower has little to do with its growth. Once sown, the farmer must wait for natural and unknown processes to work. He "sleeps and rises night and day." "The seed sprouts and grows; he knows not how" (v. 27). The most essential aspects of the seed's growth remain outside the sower's knowledge or control. Germination and growth occur without the sower's help. "The growth process is summarized: "The earth produces by itself, first the blade, then the ear, then the full grain in the ear."

Once growth and production have occurred, harvest occurs. This kingdom parable illustrates that God's ordained way of growth will happen through God's sovereign administration. God will continue to grow the ranks of those who will be included in the kingdom's elite leadership. Once satisfied, God will initiate the harvest, which permanently transitions the physical manifestation of ruling authority from heaven to earth.

The Parable of the Mustard Seed

And he said, "With what can we compare the kingdom of God, or what parable shall we use for it? It is like a grain of mustard seed, which, when sown on the ground, is the smallest of all the seeds on earth, yet when it is sown it grows up and becomes larger than all the garden plants and puts out large branches, so that the birds of the air can make nests in its shade." (Mark 4:30–32)

Mark's third and final kingdom parable is also a "seed" parable. The parable of the mustard seed is among the very few parables to occur in the Gospels of Matthew, Mark, and Luke. Most focus on peculiarities that exist between these three accounts.

However, the point of the parable is not difficult to understand. A grain of mustard seed begins very small but ends larger than all garden plants. France correctly captures the point of comparison when he writes, "It is this contrast between an insignificant beginning and an impressive final size which is the point.[98]

In one sense, God's sovereign administration began with the king's birth. By all earthly standards, this birth was unremarkable. Even with the angelic accompaniment, few knew anything about it. Those who did were challenged in everything they had come to expect. With the birth of one child who, in the world's view, was unimportant, the sovereign administration or royal rule of God had begun.

For more than thirty years, nothing seemingly happened. Then Jesus, the God-Man, began calling men and women to join him in pursuing the lofty goal of earning elite status in the coming rule of God on earth. Though then (as now), men overwhelmingly rejected God's offer, the ranks will grow. When God ultimately completes the court of his royal house leadership, a permanent physical manifestation of heaven's rule will come to earth. At that time, God will have answered the prayer of the ages: "Thy kingdom come, thy will be done on earth as it is in heaven." The Lord Jesus will sit on his glorious throne, and those who earned the right to join him will do the same.

The whole world will submit to his rule. What was once a kingdom of one baby boy born into the dirt and grime of a stranger's stable will become the ruler of all creation. This is genuinely a mustard seed story, if there ever was one!

CHAPTER 9

Where Is My Seat?

In the Gospel of Matthew, the mother of the sons of Zebedee comes to Jesus with a request for her two boys. The text records,

> Then the mother of the sons of Zebedee came up to him with her sons, and kneeling before him she asked him for something. And he said to her, "What do you want?" She said to him, "Say that these two sons of mine are to sit, one at your right hand and one at your left, in your kingdom." Jesus answered, "You do not know what you are asking. Are you able to drink the cup that I am to drink?" They said to him, "We are able." He said to them, "You will drink my cup, but to sit at my right hand and at my left is not mine to grant, but it is for those for whom it has been prepared by my Father." (Matt. 20:20–23)

To many readers of the New Testament, this mother's question may be unsettling. Who would have the audacity to ask Jesus such a thing? But her question must not surprise us. Since our Lord began to shout out loud the good news from God, the most probative question on the minds of the Twelve was, "Who gets what?" Clearly, positions of honor in the coming kingdom were open. How one gets one of these positions must not have been clearly defined. The Lord Jesus' aunt, the mother of James and John of Zebedee requested that her two boys sit "one at your right hand and one at your left." Would being seated in these positions be the highest honor possible?

Certainly, to be seated at the right hand of God is an exalted position. The book of Hebrews declares four times that Jesus, due to his faithfulness, received this honor: "He sat down at the right hand of the Majesty on high" (Heb. 1:3); "[Jesus] is seated at the right hand of the throne of the Majesty in heaven" (Heb. 8:1): "He [Jesus] sat down at the right hand of God" (Heb. 10:12); "[Jesus] is seated at the right hand of the throne of God" (Heb. 12:2). This is his reward for faithful service, which included his willingness to die on the cross.

The book of Hebrews reports Jesus taking this position as the fulfillment of messianic prophecy.

Specifically, Hebrews 1:13 identifies Jesus as the fulfillment of Psalm 110:1, which most scholars recognize as messianic.[99] Indeed, New Testament authors use Psalm 110 more than any other Old Testament passage.[100] The verse states, "To which of the angels has he ever said, "Sit at my right hand until I make your enemies a footstool for your feet"? This, the Hebrew writer says of the Son, Jesus Christ.

It is this, the very first verse of Psalm 110, that now draws our attention. Mark 12:35–37 states,

> As Jesus taught in the temple, he said, "How can the scribes say that the Christ is the son of David? David himself, in the Holy Spirit, declared, 'The Lord said to my Lord, "Sit at my right hand, until I put your enemies under your feet."' David himself calls him Lord. So how is he his son?"

With his response, Jesus silenced the religious leaders. Mark 12:34 states, "After that, no one dared to ask him any more questions." Jesus had put the religious leaders in a time-out. So, what is happening here?

In this passage, Jesus asked, "How can the scribes say that Christ is the son of David?" By this question, he does not deny Davidic parentage for the Christ. He is questioning the glass ceiling placed on him by the religious leaders of Israel. Logically, a son is inherently subordinate to his father. This is the normal, natural, customary way of thinking about a son. Nevertheless, such thinking ignores another aspect of the Christ as presented in the Old Testament, one that the religious leaders were missing: his lordship.

There is no explicit reference in the Old Testament to the effect that Christ is a son of David. While there may be a lack of explicit Old Testament scriptural basis to make this declaration, the same is not the case with his lordship. This is explicitly asserted in Scripture. To this very point, our Lord directs the scribes and others in the temple to consider. Our Lord asks, "How can the scribes say that Christ is the son of David?"

Since the scribes are the experts on the actual text of Old Testament Scripture (their job was to copy it word for word), who better to ask this question than them? We can assume there is a pause after our Lord's question to allow the scribes to answer.

After receiving no reply, Jesus reports, "David himself, in the Holy Spirit, declared. . .. What Jesus is about to articulate is from the inspired mouth of King David. By emphasizing that David himself wrote these words and that the Holy Spirit inspired them, Jesus gives no wiggle room for the scribes to reject what the text says. David himself declared, "The Lord said to my Lord."

The brilliance of Jesus in saying a lot with so few words is on full display here. Every morning, the faithful practicing Jew rose to repeat the Shema: "Hear, O Israel: The Lord our God, the Lord is one," which Jesus referenced in Mark 12:29–31. Thus, every Jewish person would have recognized immediately without needing clarification that "The Lord our God" is the referent. Jesus understands the sentence to mean: "The Lord [God] said to my [David's] lord [the Christ]."

Jesus points out that David has recognized the lordship of Christ, which demands that Christ be more than a mere Davidite. In Mark 12:35–37, Jesus explicitly references Psalm 110:1 to make this point. The Christ is David's Lord. The uniqueness of Christ is evidenced by his invitation: "Sit at my right hand until I put your enemies under your feet." The exaltation of the Christ to "sit at my right hand" is far more significant than maybe first perceived.

The Right Hand: An Elevated Place of Authority

Most scholars recognize that an invitation to "sit at my right hand" suggests an elevation to a place of authority, power, and honor.[101] Used in Psalm 110:1, it connotes the unusual exaltation of David's Lord. By God's invitation, Christ assumes the most honored seat in all of creation, which speaks to his uniqueness. The implication is not subtle. When asked by the high priest at his trial, "Are you the Christ, the Son of the Blessed?" Jesus responded, "I am, and you will see the Son of Man seated at the right hand of Power and coming with the clouds of heaven." To this, the high priest tore his garments and said, "What further witnesses do we need? You have heard his blasphemy."

There are three declarative statements here: (1) "I am" the Christ; (2) "You will see the Son of Man seated at the right hand of Power"; and (3) "You will see the Son of Man...coming with the clouds of heaven." Which of these three is a blasphemous statement? None. However, in the minds of the Jewish leadership, it was all three. Nothing about Jesus satisfied their expectation of what the Christ would do or say. They did not have a problem with the Christ being seated at God's right hand. They had a problem with Jesus applying that claim—and that honor—to himself.

In neither the Old Testament nor the New Testament does anyone claim the honor of taking a seat at God's right hand, with one exception. Jesus! With honor comes authority. The Christ will exercise divine prerogatives (Rev. 2:26–27; 3:23), including being the divine cloud-rider. God as a cloud-rider is referenced several times in the Old Testament: Psalm 104:1–4, Daniel 7:13, Isaiah 19:1, and Psalm 18:9–15. Since God alone is the cloud-rider, for Jesus to claim this position was blasphemous indeed in the eyes of the religious leaders. Jesus was claiming to be God.

How much the disciples understood about Christ's coming kingdom is unclear. However, it is apparent that they fully expected roles of honor to be given to them.

The mother of John and James requested that her two sons sit one at his right hand and one at his left in the coming kingdom. These positions of honor were available, but Jesus was not the one responsible for assigning them. Nor were those positions obtained by favoritism. Instead, Jesus answered, "You do not know what you are asking. Are you able to drink the cup that I am to drink?" "To drink the cup" implies that the honor of elite status in the coming kingdom of Christ is earned. Jesus had to earn it, and so must we.

For those still skeptical, Jesus' question is very insightful. Jesus obtained his seat by enduring pain and suffering that ended with death (Matt. 26:39, 42) followed by the resurrection. The highest positions of honor in the coming kingdom must also be earned by suffering. Yet, even with a resume of suffering and death, it is the prerogative of the Father who gets the most honored seats.

It is unclear whether the disciples understood the symbolic use of "drinking the cup." This cup that Jesus was about to drink involved both suffering and death, which he would request on several occasions that the Father "remove" from him. However, there is no indication that the disciples understood this and could contextualize our Lord's meaning.[102] This awareness will come after our Lord's resurrection.

France identifies "the cup of suffering and judgment"[103] that blocks our Lord's path to glory. Evan calls it "the cup of wrath."[104] For Jesus, the metaphor of the "cup" is his death. There is no reason to believe that he did not fully comprehend what awaited him. On three previous occasions, Jesus warned the disciples that "the Son of Man would be delivered over to the chief priests and scribes, and they would condemn him to death and deliver him over to the Gentiles to be mocked and flogged and crucified." Jesus knew that his death would be painful and vicious, but he also knew that the crown of gold comes through the crown of thorns.

Thus, while the disciples might experience the same "cup" of death as Jesus did, he had no ability to assign them the two unique positions of honor they requested. He explained to his disciples that this prerogative is the exclusive domain of the Father: "To sit at my right hand and at my left is not mine to grant, but it is for those for whom my Father has prepared it."

In Mathew 19:28, in response to the rejection of Jesus by the rich young ruler (the poster child for the third soil of the parable of the sower), Jesus gave the Twelve some very interesting news. He told them,

> "Truly, I say to you, in the new world, when the Son of Man will sit on his glorious throne, you who have followed me will also sit on twelve thrones, judging the twelve tribes of Israel."

Luke 22:28–30, which parallels Matthew's account, reports,

"You are those who have stayed with me in my trials, and I assign to you, as my Father assigned to me, a kingdom, that you may eat and drink at my table in my kingdom and sit on thrones judging the twelve tribes of Israel."

Earning a kingship by suffering is modeled by Jesus' own life. It is compelling that he told the Twelve that their seats in the coming kingdom had already been determined. However, unlike the seats of greatest honor, their exaltation to the ruler status during the Lord's reign is Jesus' prerogative. The Lord answered Peter's question in Matthew 19:27: "Then Peter replied, 'See, we have left everything and followed you. What then will we have?'"

There is great irony here. If the rich young ruler had abandoned all his worldly goods and followed Christ, he would have gained far more than he had given up. He would have received the material blessings promised in this life, including elite status and rulership in the sovereign administration of God on earth, and the treasures stored up for him in heaven (Matt. 6:19–21), as well.

All of these promises are fulfilled "in the new world when the Son of Man will sit on his glorious throne." "The new world" is the expression the ESV chose to translate the Greek term *palingenesia*. The NET Bible prefers "in the age when all things are renewed." The KJV has "in the regeneration." The term is used twice in the New Testament.[105] In Matthew, it applies to the created order. In Titus 3:5, Paul applies it to men and women. In both cases, the dominant idea is new birth.

With the Twelve, Jesus inaugurated the divine campaign to build his leadership constituency for the eventual physical manifestation of the divine rule of God on earth. All subsequent followers of Jesus are also offered the opportunity to earn an elite leadership position in his coming royal rule by suffering. Therefore, it is critical that disciples understand when rewards will be given and exercised.

Matthew 19:28 explicitly tells us when this vital transition will occur in the sequence of end-time events. As previously stated, Peter asks literally, "What then shall be to us?" Jesus explains, "Truly, I say to you all. . .." Jesus is speaking to the Twelve, which includes Judas. Jesus continues, "Truly, I say to you all that you all who have followed [aorist participle] me . . .." Notice the aspect highlighted here. First, Jesus is speaking only to the Twelve. There is no application beyond this because there are only twelve tribes of Israel.

Second, Jesus speaks of the history of the "followship" of the Twelve to this moment. He grants subordinate kingships to the Twelve based on their behavior: "You are those who have stayed with me in my trials, and I assign to you, as my Father assigned to me, a kingdom, that you may eat and drink at my table in my kingdom and sit on thrones judging the twelve tribes of Israel" (Luke 22:28–30).

Therefore, before their deaths, the Twelve knew that they would reign with Christ as kings. It is our conviction that human history as we know it will end with the final week of Daniel's prophecy concerning the last seven years of Gentile dominance over the Jews and Jerusalem (Dan. 9:24–27). With the last blast of God's wrath against Satan, the beast, and the beast-marked worshippers in the form of seven bowl judgments, which devastate the physical earth, God will renew the earth for the reign of his Son, Jesus.

CHAPTER 10

Will There Be Crying at the Bema Seat?

Most New Testament scholars insist on merging the good news from God and the good news about Jesus Christ, confusing virtually every page. Passages that speak of sanctification are confused with passages about salvation. For some, any suggestion of loss of salvation due to unfaithfulness only proves that the person was never saved in the first place (Calvinism). For others, it demonstrates that a person can be saved for a while but eventually lose his or her salvation due to unfaithfulness (Arminianism).

The idea that one can lose salvation due to unfaithfulness is a conclusion often drawn from the three linked parables in Matthew 24 and 25 regarding the delayed return of the master. These parables address not only the master's delay but also the consequences of being unprepared or not preparing appropriately for his return.[106] The first of these parables concerns ten virgins (Matt. 25:1–13). Once the master appears, it is too late to get ready. In the other two, Jesus focuses not on being unprepared but on not preparing *appropriately* for the master's return (Matt. 24:45–25:30; 45–55).[107]

In the first of these two servant parables, Jesus says:

> "Who then is the faithful and wise servant, whom the master has put in charge of the servants in his household to give them their food at the proper time? It will be good for that servant whose master finds him doing so when he returns. Truly I tell you, he will put him in charge of all his possessions. But suppose that servant is wicked and says to himself, 'My master is staying away a long time,' and he then begins to beat his fellow servants and to eat and drink with drunkards. The master of that servant will come on a day when he does not expect him and at an hour he is not aware of. He will cut him to pieces and assign him a place with the hypocrites, where there will be weeping and gnashing of teeth." (Matt. 24:45–51)

In the parable of the talents, Jesus says,[108]

"For it will be like a man going on a journey, who called his servants and entrusted to them his property.

To one he gave five talents, to another two, to another one, to each according to his ability. Then he went away.

"He who had received the five talents went at once and traded with them, and he made five talents more. So also he who had the two talents made two talents more. But he who had received the one talent went and dug in the ground and hid his master's money.

"Now after a long time the master of those servants came and settled accounts with them.

"And he who had received the five talents came forward, bringing five talents more, saying, 'Master, you delivered to me five talents; here, I have made five talents more.' His master said to him, 'Well done, good and faithful servant. You have been faithful over a little; I will set you over much. Enter into the joy of your master.'

"And he also who had the two talents came forward, saying, 'Master, you delivered to me two talents; here, I have made two talents more.' His master said to him, 'Well done, good and faithful servant. You have been faithful over a little; I will set you over much. Enter into the joy of your master.'

"He also who had received the one talent came forward, saying, 'Master, I knew you to be a hard man, reaping where you did not sow, and gathering where you scattered no seed, so I was afraid, and I went and hid your talent in the ground. Here, you have what is yours.' But his master answered him, 'You wicked and slothful servant! You knew that I reap where I have not sown and gather where I scattered no seed? Then you ought to have invested my money with the bankers, and at my coming I should have received what was my own with interest.

"So, take the talent from him and give it to him who has the ten talents. For to everyone who has will more be given, and he will have an abundance. But from the one who has not, even what he has will be taken away. And cast the worthless servant into the outer darkness. In that place there will be weeping and gnashing of teeth." (Matt. 25:14–30)

Based on a superficial understanding, it is easy to see why many NT scholars believe that the worthless servants in both parables either lost their salvation or never had it in the first place. Barbieri is typical of those holding to this view, as reflected in *Bible Knowledge Commentary*: "Like the unworthy servant in 24:48–51, he [the servant who buried the talent] too would be eternally separated from God."[109] Thus, in Barbieri's view, the parable of the talents is about who will be spiritually saved and who will be spiritually lost.

As long as there remains confusion about the good news from God and the good news about Jesus Christ, there will be confusion and contradiction in interpreting New Testament Scripture. Salvation is a *faith* issue. Sanctification is a *faithfulness* issue. There is only one condition on which to receive personal salvation—faith—and we fail to see how the atonement of Christ does not cover unfaithfulness (a sin) in the life of a believer. Yet countless conditions are attached to receiving heavenly rewards due to one's continued *sanctification*.

There is a similar duality when it comes to consequences. The consequence of a lack of personal salvation is eternal punishment. The result of having lived a life of carnality is loss of rewards (1 Cor. 3:15). The gospel from God calls men to live sanctified lives to turn away God's coming judgment. The gospel about Jesus Christ calls men to believe in the death, burial, and resurrection of Jesus for the forgiveness of sin (Luke 24:47).

Understanding the difference between the two gospels is imperative for correctly interpreting significant portions of the New Testament. Nowhere is this more important than in the gospels of Matthew, Mark, and Luke. There is no basis to see the death, burial, and resurrection of Jesus Christ for the forgiveness of sin controlling the meaning of these books. The good news from God dictates the meaning of these texts.

Who is the Audience?

The most probative question concerns the intended audience in determining the appropriate interpretation of the three linked parables. Understanding the audience helps us determine the speaker's intent—in this case, Jesus.

Knowing whether Jesus is talking to believers only, to both believers and unbelievers or to unbelievers only greatly influences how one interprets the parables. It is our position that he is speaking to believers here. Thus, he is speaking to an audience made up of those who already believe and are committed to following him.

By way of reminder, Luke 8:9–10 states the purpose of parables. He records,

> When his disciples asked him [Jesus] what this parable meant, he said, "To you it has been given to know the secrets of the kingdom of God, but for others they are in parables, so that 'seeing they may not see, and hearing they may not understand.'"

In other words, the purpose of speaking in parables in the public arena was to keep outsiders[110] ignorant and insiders (disciples) informed about kingdom operations and outcomes.

In Matthew 24:45–51, we have a servant who can be either "faithful and wise" or "bad." In Matthew 25:1–13, we find ten virgins. Again, five of them are wise, and five of them are foolish. Finally, in Matthew 25:14–30, we find a slave or servant again, who can be either "good and faithful" or "worthless and lazy."

Depending on one's theological presuppositions, who is represented in each parable is often predetermined before exegesis. Classical dispensational thinkers limit the text to national Israel. Barbieri's comments are typical when he writes,

> *When the Lord returns "in His glory," He will judge not only the nation Israel (as in the Parable of the 10 Virgins [vv. 1–13] and the Parable of the Talents [vv. 14–30]) but also the Gentiles.*[111]

Blomberg stands at the opposite extreme. He sees all humanity represented in this parable. He writes,

> *The "three characters" are thus the master, the two good servants taken together, and the wicked servant. The final reckoning scene again refers to the final judgment that all people will undergo as they give account to God for what they have done with their lives.*[112]

Between Barbieri's view that the parable's application is limited to Jews only and Blomberg's view that it extends to all mankind is Nolland. He gives an abbreviated analysis of the historical interpretation of the one-talent servant. Noting the different positions of various authors, Nolland states:

> *Does the slave who buried the talent stand for those who fail to manifest the virtues of fidelity and effort (Jülicher), or those who preserve the Jewish tradition but make no profitable use of it for God (Jeremias), or the fearful legalists (Dupont), or those who will not make fruitful for God what Jesus brings (in various forms, Weiser, Weder, Didier), or the scribes and Pharisees, who see Jesus' God as too demanding (Lambrecht), or those who when faced with the challenge of the message of the kingdom of God, with its call to a bold readiness to risk all, take refuge in a sterile security (Puig i Tàrrech)?*[113]

Where do we stand on these parables? We recognize that care must be taken not to force parables to say more than the author intended. At the same time, we maintain that their purpose was to enlighten insiders ("those around him with the twelve, Mark 4:10). Our view (and one that escapes most readers) is that the Olivet Discourse (Matt. 24–25) was given to Peter, James, John, and Andrew (Mark 13:3). These parables were spoken to insiders—believers in the kingdom message of Jesus. This is critical to understanding their meaning.

10 Reasons the "Servants" Are Disciples

Ten reasons support the view that the servants in these parables are disciples (insiders). Thus, as parables spoken to disciples about disciples, the meaning of these parables cannot relate to the issue of spiritual salvation but rather sanctification. We will take a look at the reasons for this here.

Matthew's parable of the Talents is a kingdom parable, and most New Testament scholars agree. As such, it reveals a principle or principles of the kingdom of God. In the kingdom parables, the Lord Jesus teaches five things: (1) how the kingdom started; (2) how the kingdom grows;

(3) how the kingdom transitions from the temporal phase to the eternal phase; (4) who the constituents of the kingdom are; and (5) how to earn rewards in the coming kingdom.

At this point, we are concerned with the identity of the constituents of the kingdom. In the parable of the talents, the master "called his servants and entrusted to them his property." Here are ten reasons that we believe all three "servants" represent disciples (spiritually saved):

1. The Olivet Discourse was given to disciples who, if fortunate to be alive on the earth at the consummation, must live in constant readiness for the Son of Man's return (Matt. 24:3) to avoid negative consequences at the harvest judgment. This is the same message John the Baptist preached during his earthly ministry.

2. Matthew 25:13 is a call for watchfulness. A second-person plural imperative is used here. The subject of our Lord's command is his disciples, both those sitting in front of him and those of us who would read his words later.

3. Matthew 25:14 identifies the servants as belonging to the master. It is inconceivable that the master would trust strangers or non-servants to manage his property. The servants' call is faithfulness in discharging their responsibilities while the master is away.

4. The purpose of parables was to limit "insider information"[114] to those who continued to walk with Jesus as disciples. Outsiders, who could be either disciples or critics, were kept ignorant of the secrets of the kingdom of God. How would an unbeliever be expected to be faithful to what he is ignorant of?

5. The reason the one-talent servant hid the master's property until he returned was fear. Jesus urges his disciples not to hide their light (Matt. 5:14-15) and their faith (John 12:42; 19:38). The one-talent servant prepared for his master's return, but sadly, not correctly. This does not prove that the servant is lost, only that he is lazy and unwise.

6. Upon the master's return, servants can expect a call to account for their service following his delayed return. Subsequent NT revelation reveals several judgments connected with this event. Theological presuppositions force this parable to apply to rapture positions. However, the parable of the talents does not specify when, during the end-time sequence, the master's servants will give an account. We only know that an accounting will occur.

7. There is no indication that the "servants" are anything other than servants. In other words, the master never doubted their identity. The issue is not who they are but their faithfulness during his absence.

8. Each servant is explicitly stated to have been given talents "according to his ability." *Dynamis* (power or might) is used in Matthew 24:15, and Balz and Schneider suggest it means "ability or capability."[115] No unbeliever has the ability or capability to please God in service before salvation (Hebrews 11:6).

At the illustrative level, all three "talent" receivers are equal because they are servants. There is no indication that the servants must obtain something beyond what they already have to fulfill their mission. They already have everything they need. Therefore, the master knows enough about his servants to entrust them with his property. The idea that God entrusts kingdom knowledge to an unbeliever to carry to other unbelievers is unfathomable. There is no New Testament precedent for this notion. No unbeliever has the "ability" or "capability" to serve God faithfully before receiving the new birth.

Recognizing the need to exercise caution, we do not read the apostle Paul's writings back into Matthew but maintain doctrinal consistency across the whole of Scripture. Thirty-plus years after our Lord gave the Olivet Discourse to Peter, James, John, and Andrew, Paul makes explicit what is implied in Matthew 13:

> The natural person does not accept the things of the Spirit of God, for they are folly to him, and he is not able to understand them because they are spiritually discerned. (1 Cor. 2:14)

There is a consensus among New Testament scholars that the Greek Term *psychikós* (natural, human)[116] "means natural humanity without the eschatological gift of the Spirit."[117] Rather than accepting "the things of the Spirit of God" as truth, "they are folly to him." According to Paul, the natural person is not able to understand them.

Kistemaker and Hendriksen summarize 1 Corinthians 2:14 this way:

> *The natural man belongs to the world, while the spiritual man belongs to God. The one is an unbeliever and the other a believer; the one lacks the Spirit while the other has the Spirit; the one follows natural instincts (Jude 19), the other follows the Lord.*[118]

In our estimation, Paul's theology of man makes it impossible for any one of the servants in the parable of the talents to be an unbeliever. Why would God entrust spiritual truth to a man devoid of the Spirit, who, by definition, cannot understand the very truth entrusted? Leon Morris is right when he states, "Anyone whose equipment is only of this world, who has not received the Holy Spirit, has no ability to make an estimate of things spiritual."[119]

Thus, in the parable of the Talents, we can say that all three servants were indeed *servants* in the fullest sense. All three were entrusted with the master's property. All three had the requisite ability to fulfill their obligations. All three will be judged by the same standard—production. All three will face the possibility of reward or punishment, once the master judges their life works.

9. Matthew 25:28 indicates that the one-talent servant will suffer loss at the master's reckoning. The talent is actually taken away from him. If the one-talent servant is lost, then he is never saved. Thus, what is taken away cannot be spiritual salvation. If the person is lost and never saved, what does he have to lose? Arminians would say that this person lost his salvation due to unfaithfulness. However, the loss of salvation would have occurred long before the judgment. If this were the case, it would seem (tragically) that the one-talent servant would have no clue that he or she had become lost until the reckoning. This scenario points more towards the loss of rewards than the loss of spiritual salvation. Particularly given that the talent is taken and given to another person. If the five- and two-talent servants represent those saved, giving them additional salvation at this point makes no sense.

10. It is possible for believers to suffer loss for unfaithfulness. The apostle Paul makes this point abundantly clear in 1 Corinthians 3:10–15. He says outright, "If anyone's work is burned up, he will suffer loss, though he himself will be saved, but only as through fire." While some insist that rewards are lost but no other negative consequences will follow, we warn all men to abandon this notion. The negative repercussions detailed in Matthew 25:28–30 are intended for believers. Many will be shocked at the Bema when they discover this truth!

Do the Talents Represent Knowledge of the Kingdom?

Jesus, the Son of Man, is the master who calls his disciples to behave while he is away, with the expectation of rewarding their faithfulness or punishing their unfaithfulness upon his return. The single most consistent element of Matthew 24–25 is the Son of Man's return with judgment to follow.

His return marks a defining turn in human history, and this is a crucial doctrine in the kingdom parables. Matthew, Mark, and Luke have meticulously drawn a distinct line between insiders and outsiders regarding our Lord's teachings about the kingdom. All can hear the parables, but only the insiders get the correct interpretation.

If Jesus limited kingdom understanding to insiders, why would he entrust kingdom assets to unbelievers? Why would he expect faithfulness from an unbeliever? If unbelievers do not know the kingdom, why would Jesus entrust them with kingdom assets? No unbeliever is rewarded with salvation for faithfulness to God's law. There is no evidence that "chaff" ever becomes "wheat." There is no evidence that "not my sheep" becomes "my sheep." Yet, some insist that Jesus gives unbelievers kingdom assets and holds them responsible for faithfulness.

Understanding what the "talent" represents in this parable proves false. Parabolically speaking, a "talent" is a certain amount of money. Does it have a specific counterpart in the spiritual arena? Ben Chenoweth argues that our Lord did intend significance concerning "talent." After surveying different interpretive conclusions about the underlying referent, Chenoweth argues that the talents are "the knowledge of the secrets of the kingdom of heaven"[120] that Jesus entrusts to his disciples.

We agree that the parable of the talents is a kingdom parable.[121] Therefore, we expect to see the truth(s) of the sovereign administration of God as with other parables. However, we disagree with Chenoweth about the identity of the talents. There is no indication anywhere in Matthew, Mark, or Luke that insiders have limitations on their knowledge.[122] Nor does Chenoweth explain how knowledge can be taken away once understood. How can taking away knowledge at the end of human history be a punishment? Since the judgment in view happens at the Lord's return, it must include those resurrected. How can resurrected saints have limitations imposed on their knowledge as resurrected saints?

Five facts about the nature of a "talent" seem to limit their intended meaning. First, talent is a managed asset. Second, it is given according to a servant's ability. Third, talent can be multiplied. Fourth, a talent can be taken from one servant and given to another. Fifth, the talent never belongs to the servant.

These facts seem to rule out Chenoweth's conclusion. Taking away knowledge is not a punishment in the face of the beginning of the Lord's earthly kingdom.

Instead, we see the talent(s) as the opportunity all insiders have to earn elite status in the coming sovereign administration of God. In the future kingdom, disciples can gain positions of honor that include (1) kingships (Matt. 19:28), (2) inheriting eternal life [a qualitative issue] (Matt. 19:29),[123] (3) a hundredfold inheritance (Matt. 19:29), first-place status (Matt. 19:30), eating bread in the kingdom of God (Luke 14:15), and kingdom fellowship (Luke 13:26).[124] These are rewards for faithfulness—unfaithfulness results in the loss of kingdom privileges.

If, as we maintain, every kingdom parable conceals a secret(s) of the sovereign administration of God, then the parable of the talents must convey an essential secret. Our position is that talent represents the opportunity to earn status or positions of honor in this royal rule. The crucial question does not concern who is ruled over but who rules. All disciples are assured opportunities to earn elite status in the coming kingdom. Faithful disciples will receive opportunities to serve the master during the kingdom, but unfaithful disciples will lose their opportunities to live and work with the master during that time.

Disciples' Singular Focus

The essential goal of disciples relative to the coming kingdom (i.e., elite status) should be the singular focus of our lives (Matthew 6:33). All disciples should be committed to the singular goal of ruling and fellowshipping with Christ in this kingdom. Ruling with Christ must be earned. Every disciple has the opportunity. One's production will evidence the depth of one's devotion. Maximum production will receive the highest awards. No production will result in loss of kingdom status and isolation.

The kingdom principle regarding rewards is expressed in Matthew 25:29, which states,

> "For to everyone who has will more be given, and he will have an abundance. But from the one who has not, even what he has will be taken away."

With minor changes, this verse is the same as Matthew 13:12. This saying appears in a parallel section of Mark 4:25 and Luke 8:18, 19:26. This kingdom principle is an essential insight for insiders. It is first enunciated by the Lord Jesus in connection with the parable of the sower and then with the parable of the talents. In both parables, this enigmatic saying occurs in connection with judgment. It explains why the faithful will be given more responsibility during our Lord's kingdom rule, and the unfaithful will be reduced to worthlessness (no fellowship with the King). Faithfulness will be rewarded. Unfaithfulness will be punished with loss of kingdom status and the freedom to travel.

The punishment for unfaithfulness is expressed in Matthew 25:26a, 28, 30. Together, these verses say,

"But his master answered him, 'You worthless and slothful servant...So take the talent from him and give it to him who has the ten talents...And [he] cast the worthless servant into the outer darkness. In that place there will be weeping and gnashing of teeth.'"

These three statements lead many Bible students to conclude that the one-talent servant is not a believer. However, the reasoning is faulty. Instead of the positive commendation given to the previous servants, the one-talent servant has criticism to look forward to: "You worthless and slothful servant." In an overwhelming majority of modern translations, the term $\pi o\nu\eta\rho\acute{o}\varsigma$ is translated as either "wicked" or "evil." Louw-Nida suggests four possible nuances of this term: (1) wicked, (2) worthless, (3) guilty, and (4) sick.[125] The first nuance BADG suggests is "pertaining to being morally or socially worthless, wicked, evil, bad, base, worthless, vicious, degenerate.[126] Coupled with the adjective lazy or idle; we support the nuance "worthless." Worthlessness and laziness capture the sense of criticism. The one-talent servant produced nothing, proving his laziness and worthlessness.

This better explains the master's evaluation of his servant. The master would not have entrusted his talent to a servant who, by nature, was wicked. To expect anything other than the resulting outcome would have shown a lack of wisdom on the part of the master. In our opinion, to condemn an evil man for being evil offers no new insight into this or any of the other parables.

The second negative consequence for the unfaithful one-talent servant is the loss of opportunity to serve in the Lord's kingdom. Instead of being elevated to greater responsibility, he receives a demotion. The text says, "So take the talent from him and give it to him who has the ten talents" (Matt 25:28). This verse alone should be sufficient evidence that salvation is not in view here. No person will appear before Christ saved only to lose salvation because of insufficient funds in his or her account.

The fact that the "talent" can be given, taken back, and transferred to another significantly limits what the talent is. Old Testament history is filled with accounts demonstrating the transfer of inheritance rights due to misbehavior. Both Esau and Ruben are poster children for this. Hebrews 12:15–17 says of Esau:

See to it that no one fails to obtain the grace of God; that no "root of bitterness" springs up and causes trouble, and by it many become defiled; that no one is sexually immoral or unholy like Esau, who sold his birthright for a single meal. For you know that afterward, when he desired to inherit the blessing, he was rejected, for he found no chance to repent, though he sought it with tears.

The writer of the Book of Hebrews expresses Esau's reaction with the phrase, "he sought it with tears." Genesis 27:34 offers a more graphic depiction. Notice, "As soon as Esau heard his father's words, he cried out with an exceedingly great and bitter cry." At the critical point, repentance and weeping were insufficient to restore Esau's firstborn inheritance status. Esau never lost his sonship, but he did lose the rights and privileges of the firstborn.

Similarly, Reuben, Jacob's firstborn, also lost all rights and privileges of being the firstborn son. 1 Chronicles 5:1–2 reports:

> The sons of Reuben the firstborn of Israel (for he was the firstborn, but because he defiled his father's couch, his birthright was given to the sons of Joseph the son of Israel, so that he could not be enrolled as the oldest son; though Judah became strong among his brothers and a chief came from him, yet the birthright belonged to Joseph).

A firstborn son's honors, privileges, and rights were lost to Ruben due to his misbehavior (Gen. 35:22).

"Sons of the Kingdom"

Despite chastising them for misbehavior, Jesus is speaking to believers. Both audiences—disciples and Jews—are identified as "sons of the kingdom." Thus, Jesus rebukes those already "in the family." It is in this context that he rebukes Jewish leaders for their failure to display a faith similar to some Gentiles:

> "I tell you, many will come from east and west and recline at table with Abraham, Isaac, and Jacob in the kingdom of heaven, while the sons of the kingdom will be thrown into the outer darkness. In that place there will be weeping and gnashing of teeth."

A Handbook on the Gospel of Matthew identifies sons of the kingdom as follows: "a Semitic idiom meaning 'people (We would add here, the Jewish people) who belong to the kingdom.'"[127] Nolland identifies them as "natural heirs of the kingdom."[128] The natural heirs will suffer loss, which is recognized as the same as the one–talent servant, being "thrown into the outer darkness," where "there will be weeping and gnashing of teeth." The contrast between the faithless Jewish heirs of the kingdom and the Gentiles of faith is clear.

The talent transfer signals a loss of rights and privileges as a son of the kingdom. Regarding Matthew 8:11-12, Hagner writes:

> The allusion is to the eschatological banquet (J. Behm, TDNT 2:34–35; Str-B 4:1154–56), a great festival of rejoicing and feasting in celebration of the victory of God, anticipated in both the OT and NT (see, e.g., Isa 25:6; Matt 22:1–14; 25:10; Rev. 19:9; Luke 14:15–16; b. Pesaḥ; 119b; Exod. Rab. 25, 10).[129]

Those who fail to behave appropriately during the Lord Christ's absence will lose the right to sit and sup with him in his kingdom.

The second occurrence of the phrase "sons of the kingdom" occurs in Matthew 13:38. As Jesus explains the meaning of the kingdom parable of the weeds of the field, he identifies "the good seed" this way. Jesus, the Son of Man, sows the good seed (sons of the kingdom) in the world until the end of the age when there will be a separation in which the sons of the evil one will be removed. "Sons of the kingdom" are disciples (insiders) whose inheritance depends on their behavior.

The third and final negative consequence of the one-talent servant's unfaithfulness is restricted access to the King and his rule. Instead of gaining elite status in God's sovereign administration, with all the rights and privileges that come with it, unfaithful sons will be restricted to observance only. Instead of ruling with Christ, unfaithful disciples will be ruled over with no joy.

What Is Meant by "Outer Darkness"?

The parable of the talents concludes with a most horrifying statement: "Cast the worthless servant into the outer darkness." The adjective "worthless" (useless, worthless, unsuitable)[130] suggests that the one-talent servant no longer has any value for the master. He or she has nothing that shows glory or honor. He or she has no work and no rewards. Thus, his or her destiny is "the darkness outside."

The casting of the one-talent servant "into the outer darkness" has led some students of Scripture to conclude that this servant must be an unbeliever. We are disappointed in *A Handbook of the Gospel of Matthew* because the authors write, "*The outer darkness*, obviously [is] a reference to hell."[131] The phrase "outer darkness" occurs three times in Matthew's Gospel: 8:12, 22:13, and 25:30. Contra Balz and Schneider's conclusion: "Here σκότος refers to the eschatological place of punishment,"[132] i.e., the destiny of unbelievers.

Balz and Schneider draw a wrong conclusion here for three primary reasons. First, in the three passages of Matthew where the phrase is used, there is no mention of fire, furnace, or hell associated with "outer darkness." Of the three occasions where this phrase occurs, only those *expected to produce* for the kingdom are cast there, i.e., the sons of the kingdom who are improperly "wedding attired" or proved worthless.

On the other hand—and this is critically important—fiery punishment is only associated with those who could *never produce*, i.e., chaff, weeds, trees that produce bad fruit, goats, and evil men.

In each case, only those whose nature is consistent with their behavior are assigned to the fiery punishment. It is also worth noting that there is no change in the nature of these sons. Wheat never becomes chaff or vice versa. Good trees never become bad trees or vice versa. Sheep never become goats or vice versa. A fiery destiny is the result of one nature.

The phrase "outer darkness" does not occur with any mention of fire associated with it. "Outer darkness" is the choice of most modern translations. However, the NIV suggests a slight modification. Instead of "will be thrown into outer darkness," it suggests "will be thrown outside, into the darkness." The Greek phrase τὸ σκότος τὸ ἐξώτερον (the darkness outsidest [superlative]) taken literally would have the sense "the darkness farthest out." This view recognizes the superlative function of the adjective. Hagner suggests:

> The expression τὸ σκότος τὸ ἐξώτερον, "the outer darkness," here refers to the greatest possible contrast with the brilliantly illuminated banquet hall (cf. 22:13; 25:30; for darkness as judgment generally, see 2 Esdr 7:93; 1 Enoch 63:10; Pss. Sol. 14:4; 15:10).

Hagner uses the two other New Testament occurrences and intertestamental references to support his conclusion, which he sees as ultimately referring to the place of eternal damnation. The most exhaustive study of the phrase "outer darkness" is Marty Cauley's study *The Outer Darkness*.[133] Cauley's conclusion is probably close to Dillow, who concludes:

> *By using the phrase "the darkness outside" rather than "outer darkness," we are freed from traditional usage that might color our thinking, enabling us to more easily discern what the phrase means in context. When we do that, it becomes highly probable that this phrase refers to the darkness outside the relative light of the banquet hall.*
>
> *Presumably, in the story, this is a local area immediately outside the banquet hall. The phrase is a metaphor for an experience of exclusion from the joy. . . . Matthew, therefore, leads us to imagine a feast of great rejoicing. All the faithful Christians of the church are there to celebrate their wedding feast with their King. This joyful banquet is portrayed by the Lord as occurring in the evening in a brightly lit banquet hall. Outside the banquet, where the shining lights of the feast are not present, in that place, the evening darkness prevails. This is a metaphor for the relative physical darkness. This darkness is not literal, but is a metaphor for the exclusion of the carnal Christian from the glorious reign of the Metochoi. It is not the darkness of eternal exclusion from heaven.[134]*

Instead of seeing the one-talent servant as an unbeliever cast into the eternal lake of fire, Dillow and Cauley see a carnal Christian restricted from the sweet fellowship of the Lord Jesus and faithful disciples for a period of time.

The result of the one-talent servant being cast into the darkness outside is "weeping and gnashing of teeth." This expression occurs seven times in the New Testament (Matt. 8:12; 13:42, 50; 22:13; 24:51; 25:30; and Luke 13:28). There is one sure commonality that exists between these passages: "Weeping and gnashing of teeth" comes in response to divine judgment. Contrary to Rodney K. Duke, who states that both Matthew and Luke use this clause "in final-judgment texts,"[135] we see his comments as overly simplistic. The object of judgment and when in the sequence of the return and rule of the Son of Man a particular judgment occurs must be contextually determined. Assuming or attempting to defend only one eschatological judgment requires abandoning the consistent hermeneutic necessary in light of progressive revelation. At a minimum, Revelation 20:4–6 and 11–15 demand a thousand-year separation between the judgment of the righteous and wicked dead.

"Weeping and Gnashing of Teeth"

An oversimplified eschatology creates more problems than solutions for the overall end-times sequence. Jesus explicitly promises to return to earth and rule with his disciples.

Thus, there is significant evidence in Matthew, Mark, and Luke that the wicked living at that time will be removed from the earth. These judgments are pronounced upon the living. In order for them to apply to the evil, the wicked would need to have been resurrected. Yet in not a single parable of the kingdom is there an explicit basis for the claim that the wicked dead will experience resurrection before their judgment leading to eternal fire as reflected in the White Throne Judgment of Revelation 20:11–15.

In the seven passages that use the idiom "weeping and gnashing of teeth," those suffering are alive and judged. Again, we see no evidence of an immediate resurrection associated with any judgment scene in these passages.

There is nothing uniquely Christian or unchristian about the idiom "weeping and gnashing of teeth" (Matt. 8:12; 13:42, 50; 22:13; 24:51; 25:30; and Luke 13:28). Matthew 13:42, 50 applies it to unbelievers, while Matthew 8:12, 22:13, 24:51, 25:30, and Luke 13:28 apply to disciples. The phrase in and of itself is a reaction to the sentence of judgment. Once the sentence is completed, the one-talent servant reacts with "weeping and gnashing of teeth."

The term for weeping occurs twice in the New Testament outside the end-time passages under review. Matthew 2:8 speaks of Rachel weeping for her children, which refers to Jeremiah's record of events connected with the Babylonian captivity. Slaughtering innocent babies would cause moms to wail over the death of their children.

A second, more interesting example occurs in Acts 20:37. During the occasion of Paul's farewell to the Ephesian elders, the text reports:

> And there was much weeping on the part of all; they embraced Paul and kissed him, being sorrowful most of all because of the word he had spoken, that they would not see his face again.

The cause of "much weeping" is "being sorrowful most of all that they would not see" Paul's face again. The Ephesians experienced great anxiety concerning Paul's departure. Their sorrowful regret was on display for all to see.

In many cases, "loud laments" are paired with the "gnashing of teeth." We agree with McComiskey, who argues that this phrase's rare appearance and usage in secular Greek and Jewish literature should cause New Testament interpreters to seek a precise meaning from each passage and its immediate context.[136]

While the individual words are essential, the significance of our study is the idiom itself. Whether this idiom is an invention of the Lord Jesus or a common speak of his day is unknown. Erdey and Smith, in their article "Weeping and Gnashing of Teeth: The Nature of the Suffering of the Wicked in Matthew," conclude as follows:

> *The three concepts associated with the phrase "weeping and gnashing of teeth," namely, "outer darkness," "fiery furnace," and "dismemberment" . . . may help to provide the essential context required for understanding such a unique Matthean passage, without verbal or conceptual precedent on which to rely for accurate interpretation.[137]*

We believe the phrase the "darkness outside" refers to the abode of unfaithful disciples during Christ's thousand-year rule on earth. It is the punishment for those who refuse to live repentant lives before our Lord's return. These will lose all rights and privileges of sonship.

The "fiery furnace" refers to the abode of the living wicked once judged at the return of the Son of Man. In the parable of the wheat and weeds, the destiny of the weeds (those who belong to Satan) is removed from the earth and thrown alive into the fiery furnace. The weeds were never wheat nor vice versa.

The third group, identified as those who will weep and gnash their teeth, is seen in Matthew 24:51: "He will cut the servant to pieces." This describes the result for those who are found unfaithful at the Lord's return. Taken at face value, many scholars automatically see dismemberment as a judgment that results in eternal damnation. Duke uses this verse to bolster his claim that those thrown out of the kingdom are not the ones who weep and gnash their teeth. Duke calls for restraint when considering what conclusions, one should draw from metaphorical language in these passages.[138]

Yet, Duke violates his rule here because he does not restrain himself from drawing a conclusion that needs a better defense. To cut the servant into pieces can just as easily be taken metaphorically as literally. Suppose literal death by dismemberment is the punishment for unfaithful servants. In that case, this passage alone teaches such a conclusion. Rather, we better interpret this as symbolic since nowhere else in Scripture is physical death, the eternal punishment of the wicked. Those judged and thrown into the everlasting fire in Matthew 25:41 never experience physical death but are thrown into the fire alive.[139]

What About 'No More Tears'?

If, as we insist, unfaithful believers will suffer profound regret after receiving their punishment, then we must explain Revelation 7:17, which affirms, "God will wipe away every tear from their eyes." Likewise, Revelation 21:4 also promises, "He will wipe away every tear from their eyes, and death shall be no more, neither shall there be mourning, nor crying, nor pain anymore, for the former things have passed away."

Of the two, the less complicated text to explain is Revelation 21:4. If one accepts, as we do, the chronological development of Revelation 19–21:8, the promises contained in Revelation 21:4 find fulfillment once the thousand-year reign of Christ has finished. The eternal future of mankind begins (following the creation of a new heaven and earth [Rev. 21:1]). Once humanity is past the temporal reign of Christ on earth, the Sovereign of all glory will rule over the totality of creation. For righteous people, in his eyes, all characteristics and reminders of this fallen world will pass away. Thus, the tears that are wiped away are those associated with death, mourning, and pain. Yet, one must agree that these are not the sole producers of tears in believers' lives. Believers will also experience tears of joy and tears shed over the loss of loved ones who did not make it into the camp of the saved.

Our understanding of Revelation 7:17 is more nuanced. Without dealing at length with the chronology of the book of Revelation and whether there is a recapitulation in some sections, we see Revelation 7 preceding the physical manifestation of God's sovereign administration on earth. The context limits the audience to those "coming up out of the great tribulation," where persecution, murder, violence, and pain have ruled for several years.

Scholars recognize, whether directly or indirectly, that in verse 17, John alludes to Isaiah 25:8. The promise to "wipe away tears from all faces" must be contextually defined. In Isaiah 25:8 and Revelation 7:17, the promise of no more tears is connected with alleviating death and suffering. After promising those "coming up out of the great tribulation" that they will hunger or thirst no more, Revelation 7:17 adds the promise that the Lamb "will guide them to springs of living water." Thus, this must refer to spiritual water or the endless supply of eternal life because the text informs the reader that there will be no need to drink water or eat food. Yet, there will be eating and drinking during the Lord's kingdom on earth (see Mark 14:25).

Thus, we must limit the cessation of tears associated with death and dying only. Tears associated with shame, regret, joy, and powerful aesthetic experiences like the sudden appearance of the Lord Jesus, the glorious throne of the Father, or the New Jerusalem are not removed.

We see no necessity to include in this promise tears of joy, tears of relief, or tears of accomplishment. Contextually, to see a blanket ban on tears of any kind seems unwarranted and overly simplistic.

CHAPTER 11

Training to Reign: Suffer Well!

By recognizing the fundamental distinction between the gospel from God and the gospel about Jesus Christ, we have demonstrated how many problematic passages in the Gospels are resolved. Instead of seeing at least one offer of spiritual salvation on every page, we see our Lord focused on the coming rule of God on the earth and the unique opportunity disciples have been given to participate in his ruling cabinet.

The gospel of the kingdom of God announces God's intent to grant his Son authority to rule over the earth and invites the disciples to share in that kingdom's rule. It also announces that judgment awaits those who refuse to live a repentant life. God's sovereign administration will consist of the Lord Jesus and the men and women who *earn* the right to rule with him. Ruling with Christ is a reward. The primary avenue that will lead to this reward is *suffering!*

Suffering—the Divine Imperative

Every man, woman, boy, or girl who hopes to take part in the coming rule of God upon the earth must acquire that honor through suffering. There are no exceptions. In this, Jesus Christ was our model. The suffering of our Savior was not theoretical nor limited to the spiritual arena. He predicted "that he must go to Jerusalem and suffer many things from the elders and chief priests and scribes, be killed, and on the third day be raised" (Matt. 16:21, ESV, emphasis added). Jesus predicts that he, himself, must suffer. This verb, often translated in the New Testament as "must," is generally understood to indicate a divine imperative.

In essence, Jesus's suffering was God's explicit and unalterable will. W. J. Bennett, Jr. concludes that this verb is another way of saying, "God wills it." The suffering of the Lord Jesus is explicitly predicted in Old Testament Scripture, thus

119

the absolute necessity of its fulfillment (Luke 24:46). The question is, why? Why was it an absolute necessity that the Son of God suffer in the flesh? Hebrews 2:10 tells us.

The writer states, "For it was fitting that he [God the Father], for whom and by whom all things exist, in bringing many sons to glory, should make the founder [Jesus Christ] of their salvation perfect through suffering." What does the writer mean by "perfect through suffering?" We categorically affirm that the Lord Jesus had no moral imperfections (2 Cor. 5:21), yet Scripture affirms that Jesus grew in wisdom, knowledge, and favor with God and man (Luke 2:52).

Our Lord's growth in "wisdom, knowledge, and favor" helps us understand what the writer of Hebrews means by "perfect through suffering." We agree with Silva that the focus is "two successive stages in" the Lord's "human-messianic existence."[140] The writer of Hebrews makes a critical point regarding the significant difference between the pre-and post-resurrection Jesus. Silva highlights that Hebrews 1:4 tells us that

> God's Son has inherited a name superior to that of the angels. But when we ask what is the name that this Son has inherited, the answer is, oddly enough, Son again (verses 5ff.). It is, I think, surprising that very little has been made in the past of the apparent fact that the author uses the word Son in two different senses in these verses. In verse 2 it indicates what Jesus is, and has always been, by divine nature; in verses 4ff. it is the Messianic title He receives in connection with some type of change in his human nature. Surely this temporal distinction—that after completing his work Jesus became something he was not before—accords naturally with the context.[141]

The writer of Hebrews distinguishes two phases of our Lord's life by stating, "We see him [Jesus] who for a little while was made lower than the angels, namely Jesus, crowned with glory and honor because of the suffering of death" (Heb. 2:9). For Jesus, perfection was the attainment of the *status* and *statue* that were the intent of his incarnation. His resurrection finalized his human experience. Suffering unto death fulfilled the experiential necessity of the God-Man knowing the total sense of his human side.

The verb in Matthew 16:31 is paschō, to *suffer* (death).[142] It occurs no less than 42 times in the NT, with 35 of those occurrences referring to either the Lord Jesus or his followers. On two subsequent occasions, the Lord will describe the type of suffering he will endure at the hands of the Jew in Jerusalem. This verb is the only explicit term for suffering in connection with Jesus in the Synoptic Gospels. (See Matthew 16:21, par. Mark 8:31/Luke 9:22; Matthew 17:12, par. Mark 9:12/Luke 17:25; Luke 22:15 and 24:26, 46.)

The depth of physical suffering our Lord endured is hard to grasp. The Synoptics seem to go out of their way to portray his physical suffering in the most graphic way possible. It is to this end that all disciples of Jesus Christ are called. The Lord Jesus states in Matthew 16:24: "If anyone would come after me, let him deny himself and take up his cross and follow me." A cross has only one purpose—to inflict pain and suffering that leads to physical death.

Disciples Must Suffer

The Lord Jesus explicitly tells his disciples, "In the world, you will have tribulation" (Jo 16:33). He reserves this term to describe their future experience. The same verb is used by the apostle Paul in Ac 14:22, where he declares that "through many tribulations, we must enter the kingdom of God." It is as much the will of God that disciples endure "many tribulations" as it was for Jesus. The same verb occurs here as it does in connection with the Lord's prediction in Matt 16:31. Both Jesus' suffering and his disciples are divine requirements.

Paul describes the suffering all disciples are called to endure: "tribulation." Balz and Schneider state, "The noun...is always (45 NT occurrences) used in the fig(urative) sense in the NT."[143] Louw and Nida define it to mean "trouble involving direct suffering— 'trouble and suffering, suffering, persecution.'"[144] John 16:21 illustrates this noun when it states,

> When a woman is giving birth, she has sorrow because her hour has come, but when she has delivered the baby, she no longer remembers the anguish [tribulation] for joy that a human being has been born into the world.

As with Jesus, we ask, "Why is suffering necessary?" Previously, we demonstrated that in Acts 14:22, Paul's point referred to participating in the divine leadership of God's coming rule. This is confirmed in his letter to the Romans. In the most straightforward presentation of the theological basis for the gospel of God (Rom. 1:1), Paul reminds his readers:

> For you did not receive the spirit of slavery to fall back into fear, but you have received the Spirit of adoption as sons, by whom we cry, "Abba! Father!" The Spirit himself bears witness with our spirit that we are children of God, and if children, then heirs—heirs of God and fellow heirs with Christ, provided we suffer with [συμπάσχω = sympaschō] him in order that we may also be glorified with him. (Rom. 8:15–17 ESV, emphasis added)

Again, if we assume that the New Testament is always referencing spiritual salvation versus damnation at every turn, then Romans 8:15–17 is but another of many passages caught up in the fight between Calvinism and Arminianism because of the apparent necessity of works to be saved. Is our salvation dependent on our suffering? What is the relationship between suffering and spiritual salvation? How much suffering is necessary to pass the test? By insisting that every New Testament passage teaches spiritual salvation or damnation as the only two options, students must wrestle with reconciling the unreconcilable. Otherwise, salvation must ultimately be obtained by works. This is an untenable conclusion for those who insist that spiritual salvation is received by faith alone. Instead, we see Jesus offering men a "talent" (opportunity) to earn elite status in the ruling class of his coming kingdom.

If we adopt that the Greek conjunction means "if, as is the fact," as the proper sense Paul intends, then we must conclude that all believers share in Christ's suffering. How can this be possible? Is suffering, in this case, limited to the spiritual arena only? Is Paul speaking metaphorically? Similarly, we must conclude that all believers will share in his glory. Really? For this to be true, how a disciple lives his or her life has no bearing on rewards.

The NET Bible states the grammatical basis that drives many who hold this conclusion. Romans 8:17 reads: "And if children, then heirs (namely, heirs of God and also fellow heirs with Christ)—if indeed we suffer with him so we may also be glorified with him."

The NET Bible explains this translation: "On the one hand, heirs of God; on the other hand, fellow heirs with Christ." Some prefer to render verse 17: "And if children, then heirs—that is, heirs of God. Also, fellow heirs with Christ if indeed we suffer with him so we may also be glorified with him." Such a translation suggests two distinct inheritances: one coming to God's children and the other to those who suffer with Christ. However, the difficulty of this view is that it ignores the conjunctions *men...de*, "on the one hand...on the other hand." The construction strongly suggests that the inheritances cannot be separated since both explain "then heirs." For this reason, the preferred translation puts this explanation in parentheses.[145]

The grammatical conclusion that forms the basis of the NET Bible's claim is untrue. The conjunctions can indicate comparison or contrast between two or more objects. The correct technical terms are disjunctive or conjunctive. Is Paul's intent to show that "heir of God" and "co-heir of Christ" are disjunctive=contrast (i.e., a difference), or is his intent to show a conjunctive relationship=comparison (i.e., equality)? These conjunctions occur in 13 passages in the book of Romans.[146]

Setting aside Romans 8:17, the remaining passages are all contrastive (indicating a difference) and not conjunctive.

Now, this alone does not prove that Romans 8:17 is contrastive. However, one must show that this passage is distinct from all the others. The point of contrast seems to be that the difference between being an heir of God and being a co-heir with Jesus Christ is that co-heirship with Christ must be earned by suffering.

Paul is not teaching that believers share in the Lord's suffering in a symbiotic sense. While it is true that believers benefit from the death of Christ, Paul calls upon all believers to physically suffer to earn the right to join him in the administration of his coming kingdom. In Acts 14:22, Paul teaches "that through many tribulations [*thlipsis*] we must enter the kingdom of God."

Equally, Paul adds in 2 Timothy 3:12: "Indeed, all who desire to live a godly life in Christ Jesus will be persecuted." Is Paul stating an explicit prophecy here? Or is this a generalization that may or may not apply to every single believer throughout all time?

George W. Knight is representative of those who believe that the phrase, "all who desire to live godly in Christ Jesus," is not a designation of a subgroup of Christians who desire a godlier life but rather a description of genuine Christians in distinction from those who follow false teaching.[147] In contrast, we believe the key to Paul's intent is the phrase "in Christ Jesus." Paul is not saying that all believers will be persecuted just because they are believers. Instead, his emphasis is on living a godly life in Christ Jesus. Mounce concludes, "Paul is saying that everyone wishing to live a godly life, specifically Christian godliness, will be persecuted."[148] Thus, it is a subgroup that can count on persecution. Consequently, we see Romans 8:17 perfectly accord with Acts 14:22b and 2 Timothy 3:12.

Therefore, we separate "heir of God" and "co-heir with Christ." Being an heir of God is obtained by faith in the promise, which brings God's righteousness to a sinner. In Galatians 4:7, Paul states, "So you are no longer a slave, but a son, and if a son, then an heir through God." Notice the absence of conditionality. There is agreement among NT scholars that Galatians 4:7 is a direct parallel with Romans 8:17. Thus, the lack of a reference to the conditional co-heirship with Christ is significant. In Galatians 3:29, Paul argues, "If you are Christ's, then you are Abraham's offspring, heirs according to promise." Paul is referring to spiritual salvation. For Paul, being "in Christ" makes a believer an adult son and heir of God. Heirship to God has only one condition, i.e., faith in the promise of God, just as we see in Abraham.

However, co-heirship with Christ is multi-conditional, not on faith alone, but on suffering. Revelation 3:21 informs us, "The one who conquers will sit with Christ on his throne."[149] The conditionality is stated more forcefully in Revelation 2:26, which states, "The one who conquers and who keeps my works until the end, to him I will give authority over the nations." Notice the multi-conditionality!

Romans 8:17 protects salvation by faith and rewards by faithfulness by separating God's heirship and Christ's co-heirship. Rather than the unfortunate conclusion drawn by the NET Bible, the ESV maintains a theologically accurate translation of the verse. We see no less than two reasons to maintain two distinct heirships in Romans 8:17—heirs of God by faith and co-heirs of Christ by faithfulness. First, recognizing the separation between God's heirship and Christ's co-heirship removes the unnecessary appearance of a works-based salvation. Second, identifying the separation emphasizes how disciples live after putting their initial faith in Jesus Christ for spiritual salvation.

What Suffering Brings Eternal Rewards?

If co-heirship with Christ requires suffering, we must show what type of suffering is required. Of the 45 occurrences of the Greek term for "tribulation," none includes a list of examples of tribulation in the New Testament. The closest examples of what can be potentially labeled "tribulation" occur in Hebrews 10:32-34. Here, the writer details a difficult season his audience experienced. The text states,

> But recall the former days when, after you were enlightened, you endured a hard struggle with sufferings, sometimes being publicly exposed to reproach and affliction [*tribulation*], and sometimes being partners with those so treated. For you had compassion on those in prison, and you joyfully accepted the plundering of your property, since you knew that you yourselves had a better possession and an abiding one.

The author of Hebrews recounts that "you [the Hebrews] endured a hard struggle with sufferings." In essence, they endured a "contest" consisting of sufferings. Notice that the term is plural. The Hebrews were in a contest with multiple sufferings. They were publicly exposed to reproach and affliction. The Greek term for reproach is also plural and could be translated as "insults." Louw and Nida suggest "to speak disparagingly of a person in a manner which is not justified—'to insult, insult.'"[150]

The verbal insults are accompanied by *tribulation*, which is also plural. These were not one-offs but systematic patterns. If these were insufficient, the writer continues, "For you had compassion on those in prison, and you joyfully accepted the plundering of your property." There is no reason not to conclude that their (the Hebrews') imprisonment was unjustified. Lawlessness ruled.

Unlike so many who attempt to limit the NT depiction of tribulation to that final generation just before the beginning of the eschatological kingdom of God, we see every generation as having many who endure both physical and spiritual persecution because of their unwavering commitment to Jesus Christ.

In John 16:33, our Lord predicted "that in this present world, you will have affliction [*tribulation*]." Given the repeated emphasis on affliction for following Jesus, there is no need to limit our Lord's prediction to the original Twelve. In the parable of the sower, affliction is a reason given for many disciples' failings to produce fruit (Mark 4:17). Matthew records that one category of "commendables" in the coming kingdom will be those who chose to "rejoice and be glad" in the face of those "who revile and persecute, and utter all kinds of evil against" them (Matt. 5:11–12).

Repeatedly, Paul warns his converts that affliction is the constant companion of those who are serious in their *followship* of Jesus Christ. Notice how Paul intermingles Greek terms in his second letter to the Corinthians. He writes,

> Blessed be the God and Father of our Lord Jesus Christ, the Father of mercies and God of all comfort, who comforts us in all our *affliction*, so that we may be able to comfort those who are in any *affliction*, with the comfort with which we ourselves are comforted by God. For as we share abundantly in Christ's sufferings, so through Christ we share abundantly in comfort too. If we are *afflicted*, it is for your comfort and salvation; and if we are comforted, it is for your comfort, which you experience when you patiently endure the same sufferings that we suffer. Our hope for you is unshaken, for we know that as you share in our sufferings, you will also share in our comfort. For we do not want you to be unaware, brothers, of the *affliction* we experienced in Asia. For we were so utterly burdened beyond our strength that we despaired of life itself. Indeed, we felt that we had received the sentence of death. But that was to make us rely not on ourselves but on God who raises the dead. He delivered us from such a deadly peril, and he will deliver us. On him we have set our hope that he will deliver us again. (2 Cor. 1:3–10)

That which causes suffering, and the result of this suffering was evident in the lives of Paul and the Corinthians, and it will be the same for those who desire to reign with Christ in his coming kingdom. As if to underscore the reality of suffering for all believers, Paul repeats the conditions of his life as he fulfills his charge. Again, he writes:

> But we have this treasure in jars of clay, to show that the surpassing power belongs to God and not to us. We are afflicted [*thlibō*] in every way, but not crushed; perplexed, but not driven to despair; persecuted, but not forsaken; struck down, but

not destroyed; always carrying in the body the death of Jesus, so that the life of Jesus may also be manifested in our bodies. (2 Cor. 4:7–10)

We have quoted at length from the writings of the apostle Paul to encourage you not to be frightened but to count it all joy if and when the avenues of your life run through neighborhoods of affliction. It is but your *talent* (opportunity) to train to reign with Jesus Christ in the coming rule of God. No greater calling exists in the life of those who follow Jesus Christ than this:

Train Today to Reign Tomorrow!

The Gospels

The Gospel of God | Easter | The Gospel of Christ

Pre- | | Post-

Rewardific		Salvific
Faithfulness		Faith
Temporal		Eternal
Outside Darkness		Eternal Fire

Notes

[1] Matthew 13:18 says, "Hear then the parable of the sower." Thus, we identify this parable by this designation.

[2] MacArthur, J. F. (1997, 1988). *The Gospel According to Jesus: What Does Jesus Mean When He Says "Follow Me?"* Includes index. (Electronic ed.). (Grand Rapids, MI: *Academic and Professional Books*, Zondervan Pub. House).

[3] George R. Beasley-Murray, John, *Word Biblical Commentary*, Vol. 36 (Dallas: Word, Incorporated, 1999), 215.

[4] Brenda B. Colijn, "Salvation as Discipleship in the Gospel of Mark," *Ashland Theological Journal*, vol. 30 (1998), 11.

[5] Edmund K. Neufeld, "The Gospel in the Gospels: Answering the Question 'What Must I Do to Be Saved?' from the Synoptics," *Journal of the Evangelical Theological Society* 51, no. 2 (2008): 293.

[6] Based on the 28th edition of Nestle-Aland. Matthew 4:23, 9:35, 24:14, 26:13; Mark 1:1, 14, 15; 8:35, 10:29, 13:10, 14:9, and 16:15.

[7] That Luke and John never used the term is an argument from silence. However, Matthew and Mark use the term but never in direct statements of Jesus. To some degree, this is also an argument from silence.

[8] David R. Bauer, The Structure of Matthew's Gospel: A Study in Literary Design (London: Bloomsbury Academic, 1989), 73.

[9] Robertson, A. T. (2009). *A Harmony of the Gospels* (Lk 9:7–9). Logos Bible Software.

[10] https://www.churchathome.org/pdf/A%20Harmony%20of%20the%20Gospels.pdf (last accessed 8/23/23)

[11] John William McGarvey and Philip Y. Pendleton, *The Four-Fold Gospel* (Cincinnati, OH: The Standard Publishing Company, 1914), 414.

[12] Newman, B. M., & Stine, P. C. (1992). *A Handbook on the Gospel of Matthew*, United Bible Societies, 527.

[13] Johannes P. Louw and Eugene Albert Nida, *Greek-English Lexicon of the New Testament: Based on Semantic Domains* (New York: United Bible Societies, 1996), 234.

[14] Ibid., 435.

[15] Ibid., 344-345.

[16] The inauguration of the sovereign administration of the physical rule of God on earth began at the birth of Jesus and will conclude with his exaltation record in Revelation 11:15, which states, "The kingdom of the world has become the kingdom of our Lord and of his Christ and he shall reign forever and ever." The period from Christ's birth until his earthly exaltation is an open invitation to all saints to gain administrative privileges for the coming rule of God.

[17] James W. Sheets, Jr., *The Kingdom of God: The Missing Gospel within the Gospels* (LOCATION: Adonai International Christian University, 2017), 5-6.

[18] Steven R. Service, "The Lost and Forgotten Gospel of the Kingdom: A First Century Hebraic Perspective," 2nd Edition (CreateSpace Independent Publishing Platform, 2016), 5.

[19] The paraphrase *The Message* does not.

20 Chamblin, K. (1997). "*Euangelion* in Mark: Willi Marxsen Revisited." *Westminster Theological Journal*, 59(1), 34.

21 Gustavo Gutierrez, "Mark 1:14-15," *Review and Expositor*, 88 (1991), 428.

22 This is the core message of Chapter 5.

23 Kaiser, Walter C., Blaising, Craig A. *Dispensationalism, Israel and the Church: The Search for Definition* (Grand Rapids: Zondervan Publishing House, 1992), 39.

24 The grammatical formulation is different in Luke from Matthew and Mark. Luke prefers the verb εὐαγγελίζω (*euangelizō*) "to proclaim," while Matthew and Mark prefer the verb κηρύσσω (kēryssō) "to proclaim."

25 John D. Grassmick, "Mark," in *The Bible Knowledge Commentary: An Exposition of the Scriptures*, ed. J. F. Walvoord and R. B. Zuck, vol. 2 (Wheaton, IL: Victor Books, 1985), 107.

26 Scholars typically label the account that describes Jesus' explicit self-identification as the Messiah by pointing to the fulfillment of Isaiah 61:1-2a and the response of the people of Nazareth by revolting and attempting to kill him "the rejection" account.

27 Matthew 4:12 and Mark 1:14.

28 Anderson, Hugh. "Broadening Horizons: The Rejection at Nazareth Pericope of Luke 4:16-30 in Light of Recent Critical Trends," *Interpretation* 18 (1964): 260.

29 Combrink, H. J. B. (1973). "The Structure and Significance of Luke 4:16–30," *Neotestamentica*, 7, 34.

30 Walt Russell concludes:
The number of Lukan scholars who see Luke 4:16–39 in a paradigmatic or programmatic light is legion. Most significantly see Bruce Chilton, "Announcement in Nazara: An Analysis of Luke 4:16–21, " in Gospel Perspectives, Vol. 2 ed. (R. T. France and David Wenham; Sheffield: JSOT, 1981) 147–72; ed. H. Conzelman, The Theology of Luke (New York: Harper, ET 1960); H. Anderson, "Broadening Horizons," Int 18 (1964) 259-75; L. C. Crockett, "The Old Testament in the Gospel of Luke" (unpublished dissertation; Brown Univ., 1966); idem, "Luke 4:25–27 and Jewish-Gentile Relations in Luke-Acts, "JBL 88(1969) 177-183; David Hill, "The Rejection of Jesus at Nazareth," NovT 13 (1971) 161-180; and R. C. Tannehill, "The Mission of Jesus according m Luke 4:16–30, " in Jesus in Nazareth (Berlin: de Gruyter, 1972), 51-75.

Walt Russell, "The Anointing with The Holy Spirit In Luke-Acts" (1986). *Trinity Journal*, 7, 48; footnote 2.

31 Siker, J. S. (1992). "'First to the Gentiles': A Literary Analysis of Luke 4:16–30," *Journal of Biblical Literature*, vol. 111, 75.

32 Donald A. Hagner, "Matthew 1–13," vol. 33A, *Word Biblical Commentary* (Dallas: Word, Inc., 1993), 101.

33 David Hill, "The Rejection of Jesus at Nazareth," *NovT* 13 (1971), 178.

34 Bergsma, John Sietze. "The Jubilee from Leviticus to Qumran: A History of Interpretation" (Netherlands: Brill, 2007), 198.

35 The reason Judah spent seventy years in captivity in Babylon was her refusal to celebrate the year of Jubilee during her first 490 years in the land of promise.

36 Christopher R. Bruno, "Jesus is Our Jubilee . . . But How?" *JETS* 53/1 (March 2010), 95.

37 George Eldon Ladd, *The Gospel of the Kingdom* (Grand Rapids: Eerdmans, 1959), 7. This conclusion is also supported by G.R. Beasley-Murray, *Jesus and the Kingdom of Go*d (Grand Rapids: Exeter, 1986) x; B. Chilton (ed.), *The Kingdom of God* (London/Philadelphia 1984), 1.

38 Gerald F. Hawthorne, "The Essential Nature of the Kingdom of God," *Westminster Theological Journal* 25, no. 1 (1962): 35.

39 Colin H. Roberts: "The Kingdom of Heaven (Lk. XVII.21)," *Harvard Theological Review*, XLI, 1, Jan. 1948, 8.

40 C. H. Roberts, "The Kingdom of Heaven" (Lk XVII.21)," HTR 41 (1948), 1-8.

[41] G. R. Beasley-Murray, "The Kingdom of God in the Teaching of Jesus," *Journal of the Evangelical Theological Society* 35, no. 1 (1992): 23.

[42] Darrell L. Bock, "The Son of David and the Saints' Task: The Hermeneutics of Initial Fulfillment," *Bibliotheca Sacra* 150 (1993): 450.

[43] "The Kingdom of God and Ourselves," vol. 67 (1950), 172 f. (find original source material)

[44] Balz, H. R., & Schneider, G. (1990–). In *Exegetical Dictionary of the New Testament* (vol. 1, 201). (Grand Rapids, MI: Eerdmans).

[45] Ibid.

[46] Arndt, W., Danker, F. W., Bauer, W., & Gingrich, F. W. (2000). In *A Greek-English Lexicon of the New Testament and Other Early Christian Literature* (3rd ed.). University of Chicago Press, 168-169.

[47] Louw, J. P., & Nida, E. A. (1996). In *Greek-English Lexicon of the New Testament: Based on Semantic Domains* (electronic ed. of the 2nd ed., vol. 2), 44. United Bible Societies.

[48] France, R. T. (2002). *The Gospel of Mark: A Commentary on the Greek Text* (W.B. Eerdmans; Paternoster Press), 93.

[49] I. Howard Marshall, "The Hope of a New Age: The Kingdom of God in the New Testament," *Themelios* 11, no. 1 (1985): 6.

[50] G. Dalman, The Words of Jesus, Considered in the Light of Post-Biblical Writings and the Aramaic Language (Edinburgh, 1902), 91-147.

[51] Joel Marcus, "Entering into the Kingly Power of God," *Journal of Biblical Literature*, vol. 107, No. 4 (Dec, 1988), 663-664.

[52] Ibid, footnote 9.

[53] In the United States, it has become common to speak of a president's "administration" as shorthand for the president, his cabinet, and the policies that characterize his running of the country.

[54] Matthew 19:24 is parallel to Mark 10:25 and Luke 18:25. Mark 10:23 is parallel to Luke 18:24.

[55] Arndt, W., Danker, F. W., Bauer, W., & Gingrich, F. W. (2000). In *A Greek-English Lexicon of the New Testament and Other Early Christian Literature* (3rd ed., 294). University of Chicago Press.

[56] Louw, J. P., & Nida, E. A. (1996). *In Greek-English Lexicon of the New Testament: Based on Semantic Domains* (electronic ed. of the 2nd edition., vol. 1, 806–807). United Bible Societies.

[57] Matthew 22 does answer the Pharisees and elders' question about the source of the Lord's authority. It comes from his Father. The parable of the wedding feast is especially insightful (Matt. 22:1–14) in this regard.

[58] Balz & Schneider, 1990–vol. 3, 150.

[59] The traditional interpretation of the parables of the four soils is consistently misinterpreted and applied because most do not understand the difference between the good news of God and the good news of Jesus Christ.

[60] Johannes P. Louw and Eugene Albert Nida, *Greek-English Lexicon of the New Testament: Based on Semantic Domains* (New York: United Bible Societies, 1996), 807–808.

[61] Nah, D. (2018). "The Already and the Not Yet." In M. Ward, J. Parks, B. Ellis, & T. Hains (Eds.), Lexham Survey of Theology. Lexham Press.

[62] Craig A. Blaising and Darrell L. Bock, *Progressive Dispensationalism* (Wheaton: Victor, 1993), 97-98.

[63] Darrell L. Bock, "The Reign of the Lord Christ," *Dispensationalism, Israel, and the Church: The Search for Definition*, ed. by Craig A. Blaising and Darrell L. Bock (Grand Rapids: Zondervan, 1992), 37-67.

[64] Joshua, Gideon, Samson,

[65] Balz, H. R., & Schneider, G. (1990–). In *Exegetical Dictionary of the New Testament*, vol. 1 (Grand Rapids: Eerdmans), 370.

[66] Porter, S. E. (1999). *Idioms of the Greek New Testament*, 21, 22. JSOT.

[67] Guelich, R. A. (1989). "Mark 1–8:26," vol. 34A, 44. Word, Incorporated.

[68] The meaning of the phrase "to enter the kingdom of God" will be discussed in Chapter 7 of this book.

[69] John D. Grassmick, "Mark," in *The Bible Knowledge Commentary: An Exposition of the Scriptures*, ed. J. F. Walvoord and R. B. Zuck, vol. 2 (Wheaton, IL: Victor Books, 1985), 107.

[70] Lambert, David A. *How Repentance Became Biblical* (Oxford University Press. Kindle Edition), 71.

[71] Boda, Mark J. 'Return To Me': 35, *New Studies in Biblical Theology* (InterVarsity Press. Kindle Edition), 25-26.

[72] G. R. Beasley-Murray, *Jesus and the Kingdom of God* (Grand Rapids: Eerdmans; Exeter: Paternoster, 1986), 71.

[73] Most scholars agree that the Gospel of Mark establishes two major points about the Lord Jesus. Mark 1:1–8:30 proves that he is the Son of God. Mark 8:31–16:20 proves that he is the Son of Man.[73] Mark fills the first half of the book with healings, demon extractions, and short controversies with the religious leaders to prove that Jesus is God's Son. The book ends with his disciples making this exclamation. Jesus exercises authority over demons, sickness, the forgiveness of sin, the Sabbath, and the ability to appoint men to exercise divine authority, authority over death, and authority over natural law.

[74] For a defense of Matthew 13 containing eight parables, see Mark L. Bailey, "The Parable of the Sower and the Soils," *Bibliotheca Sacra* 155 (1998): 173.

[75] How many parables Mark 4 contains is debated. We do not see Mark 4:21-25 as parables proper. Given the heavy emphasis on the parables of Jesus in the Gospel of Matthew, none of the expressions found in Mark 4:21-25 is identified as a parable by Matthew. This is also the case in Luke's Gospel.

[76] A. T. Robertson, *A Harmony of the Gospels* (Bellingham, WA: Logos Bible Software, 2009), John 4:43–45.

[77] Most students of the New Testament create more problems than they understand when Judas is set aside as a bad-guy unbeliever. Most people miss the fact that Judas demonstrated the same power and ability in ministry as Peter, James, and John. There is no indication that Judas did not perform just as the others did when they went out in groups of two to preach, heal, and cast out demons. See Mark 6:12-13; Matt 10:1ff.

[78] R. T. France, The Gospel of Mark: A Commentary on the Greek Text, New International Greek Testament Commentary (Grand Rapids, MI; Carlisle: W.B. Eerdmans; Paternoster Press, 2002), 196.

[79] Ibid., 193.

[80] Ibid.

[81] Douglas S. McComiskey, "Exile and the Purpose of Jesus' Parables" (Mark 4:10–12; Matt 13:10–17; Luke 8:9–10)," *Journal of the Evangelical Theological Society* 51, no. 1 (2008): 60.

[82] Robert A. Guelich, Mark 1–8:26, vol. 34A, *Word Biblical Commentary* (Dallas: Word, Incorporated, 1989), 221. A check of many commentaries will confirm that Guelich's conclusion is shared by many scholars.

[83] Horst Robert Balz and Gerhard Schneider, *Exegetical Dictionary of the New Testament* (Grand Rapids, MI: Eerdmans, 1990–), 189. Bock, also, interprets the ἵνα (*hina*) as a purpose clause. See Darrell L. Bock, Luke: 1:1–9:50, vol. 1, *Baker Exegetical Commentary on the New Testament* (Grand Rapids, MI: Baker Academic, 1994), 734.

[84] James L. Boyer, "The Classification of Subjunctives: A Statistical Study," *Grace Theological Journal* 7, no. 1 (1986): 8.

[85] "This should not be understood as an expression for full salvation in the immediate context; it refers only to the girl's healing." This is reflected in a footnote to this verse in the NET Bible. [Biblical Studies Press, *The NET Bible First Edition*; Bible. English. NET Bible; *The NET Bible* (Biblical Studies Press, 2005).]

[86] John A. Martin, "Luke," in *The Bible Knowledge Commentary: An Exposition of the Scriptures*, ed. J. F. Walvoord and R. B. Zuck, vol. 2 (Wheaton, IL: Victor Books, 1985), 225.

[87] Johannes P. Louw and Eugene Albert Nida, *Greek-English Lexicon of the New Testament: Based on Semantic Domains* (New York: United Bible Societies, 1996), 331.

[88] Ibid., 774.

[89] For a defense of this position, see Birger Gerhardsson, *The Testing of God's Son* (Eugene: Wipf and Stock Publishers, 1966), 25ff.

[90] (1) Self-sufficiency—make bread from rocks; (2) self-preservation—prove God will save your life from death; and (3) self-exaltation—the rule of earth does not have to go through the cross.

[91] Horst Robert Balz and Gerhard Schneider, *Exegetical Dictionary of the New Testament* (Grand Rapids, MI: Eerdmans, 1990–), 248.

[92] Ibid., 409.

[93] John D. Grassmick, "Mark," in *The Bible Knowledge Commentary: An Exposition of the Scriptures*, ed. J. F. Walvoord and R. B. Zuck, vol. 2 (Wheaton, IL: Victor Books, 1985), 120.

[94] Luke 8:16–18; Matt. 5:15 and Luke 11:33; Matt. 7:2 and Luke 6:38; Matt. 10:26 and Luke 12:2; Matt. 13:12; 25:29 and Luke 19:26.

[95] Robert A. Guelich, "Mark 1–8:26," vol. 34a, *Word Biblical Commentary* (Dallas: Word, Inc., 1989), 237.

[96] James A. Brooks, "Mark," vol. 23, *The New American Commentary* (Nashville: Broadman & Holman Publishers, 1991), 84.

[97] William Hendriksen and Simon J. Kistemaker, "Exposition of the Gospel According to Mark," vol. 10, *New Testament Commentary* (Grand Rapids: Baker Book House, 1953–2001), 165.

[98] R. T. France, "The Gospel of Mark: A Commentary on the Greek Text," *New International Greek Testament Commentary* (Grand Rapids, MI; Carlisle: W.B. Eerdmans; Paternoster Press, 2002), 216.

[99] For a defense of a messianic interpretation of Psalm 110, see Herbert W. Bateman, "Psalm 110:1 and the New Testament," *Bibliotheca Sacra* 149 (1992); Barry C. Davis, "Is Psalm 110 a Messianic Psalm?" *Bibliotheca Sacra* 157 (2000): 160ff.

[100] Ibid., 160; footnote. Psalm 110 is cited in Matt. 22:44; 26:64; Mark 12:36; 14:62; Luke 20:42–43; 22:69; Acts 2:34–35; Heb. 1:13; 5:6; 7:17, 21 and alluded to in Mark 16:19; John 12:34; Rom. 8:34; 1 Cor. 15:25; Eph. 1:20; Col 3:1; Heb. 1:3; 5:10; 6:20; 7:3; 8:1; 10:12–13; 12:2.

[101] Robert G. Bratcher and Eugene Albert Nida, *A Handbook on the Gospel of Mark*, UBS Handbook Series (New York: United Bible Societies, 1993), 389; Craig A. Evans, "Mark 8:27–16:20," vol. 34b, *Word Biblical Commentary* (Dallas: Word, Inc., 2001), 273. John Aloisi, "Who Is David's Lord? Another Look at Psalm 110:1," *Detroit Baptist Seminary Journal,* vol. 10 10 (2005), 106.

[102] See Psalm 11:6; 75:8; Isa. 51:17, 22; Jer. 25:15–17, 27–28; 49:12; 51:7.

[103] R. T. France, "The Gospel of Mark: A Commentary on the Greek Text," *New International Greek Testament Commentary* (Grand Rapids, MI; Carlisle: W.B. Eerdmans; Paternoster Press, 2002), 585–586

[104] Craig A. Evans, Mark 8:27–16:20, vol. 34b, *Word Biblical Commentary* (Dallas: Word, Inc., 2001), 413. As does James A. Brooks, "Mark," vol. 23, *The New American Commentary* (Nashville: Broadman & Holman Publishers, 1991), 168.

[105] Matthew 19:28; Titus 3:5.

[106] John Nolland, The Gospel of Matthew: A Commentary on the Greek Text, New International Greek Testament Commentary (Grand Rapids, MI; Carlisle: W.B. Eerdmans; Paternoster Press, 2005), 1012.

[107] John Nolland, The Gospel of Matthew: A Commentary on the Greek Text, New International Greek Testament Commentary (Grand Rapids, MI; Carlisle: W.B. Eerdmans; Paternoster Press, 2005), 1012.

[108] Matthew 24:45-51 is not explicitly identified as a kingdom parable by Matthew; however, Luke does explicitly identify it this way (Luke 12:41). The next parable in this trilogy (the ten virgins) explicitly begins, "Then the kingdom of heaven will be like..."; thus, there is an explicit identification as a kingdom parable. The parable of the talents does not have such an explicit identification. However, Matthew 25:14 begins with grammatical indicators that signal the relationship between the parable of the ten virgins and the parable of the talents. Contra Holland and others who connect the linking $\gamma \acute{\alpha} \rho$ ('for') "to the preceding parable," as a whole, we see Matthew 25:14-30 explaining the command for watchfulness in Matthew 25:13 alone. The adverbial comparative conjunction hōsper introduces the point of the comparison between the parable of the talents and the need for watchfulness. Prepared watchfulness is the only way to ensure a pleasing life for the returning master. As well, depending on one's view of the relationship between Matthew's parable of the talents and Luke's parable of the pounds, Luke identifies his material as a parable (Luke 19:11-27).

[109] Louis A. Barbieri Jr., "Matthew," in *The Bible Knowledge Commentary: An Exposition of the Scriptures*, ed. J. F. Walvoord and R. B. Zuck, vol. 2 (Wheaton, IL: Victor Books, 1985), 80.

[110] By "unbeliever," we intend those who refuse to believe the message of Jesus concerning the kingdom of God.

[111] Louis A. Barbieri Jr., "Matthew," in *The Bible Knowledge Commentary: An Exposition of the Scriptures*, ed. J. F. Walvoord and R. B. Zuck, vol. 2 (Wheaton, IL: Victor Books, 1985), 80. See John F. Walvoord, "Christ's Olivet Discourse on the End of the Age," *Bibliotheca Sacra* 129 (1972): 210; also Samuel L. Hoyt, "The Judgment Seat of Christ in Theological Perspective Part 1: The Judgment Seat of Christ and Unconfessed Sins," *Bibliotheca Sacra* 137 (1980): 33.

[112] Craig L. Blomberg, *Interpreting the Parables, Second Edition* (Downers Grove, Il),222-223 https://www.mybibleteacher.net/uploads/1/2/4/6/124618875/interpreting_the_parables_by_craig_l._blomberg_z-lib.org_.epub.pdf (last accessed, 6/17/22).

[113] John Nolland, "The Gospel of Matthew: A Commentary on the Greek Text," *New International Greek Testament Commentary* (Grand Rapids, MI; Carlisle: W.B. Eerdmans; Paternoster Press, 2005), 1020.

[114] Ben Chenoweth, "Identifying the Talents: Contextual Clues for the Interpretation of the Parable of the Talents (Matthew 25:14-30)," *Tyndale Bulletin* 56, no. 1 (2005): 70.

[115] Horst Robert Balz and Gerhard Schneider, *Exegetical Dictionary of the New Testament* (Grand Rapids, MI: Eerdmans, 1990-), 356.

[116] Johannes P. Louw and Eugene Albert Nida, *Greek-English Lexicon of the New Testament: Based on Semantic Domains* (New York: United Bible Societies, 1996), 694.

[117] Gerhard Kittel, Gerhard Friedrich, and Geoffrey William Bromiley, *Theological Dictionary of the New Testament, Abridged in One Volume* (Grand Rapids, MI: W.B. Eerdmans, 1985), 1352.

[118] Simon J. Kistemaker and William Hendriksen, "Exposition of the First Epistle to the Corinthians," vol. 18, *New Testament Commentary* (Grand Rapids: Baker Book House, 1953-2001), 91.

[119] Leon Morris, *1 Corinthians: An Introduction and Commentary*, vol. 7, Tyndale New Testament Commentaries (Downers Grove, IL: InterVarsity Press, 1985), 64.

[120] Ibid., 70.

[121] Leon Morris, "The Gospel According to Matthew," *The Pillar New Testament Commentary* (Grand Rapids, MI; Leicester, England: W.B. Eerdmans; Inter-Varsity Press, 1992), 626-627.

[122] While we cannot say that Matthew, Mark, and Luke contain all of the parables our Lord spoke (since this is unknowable, since we cannot know what was not recorded), we can study all of the parables that *were* recorded in Scripture.

[123] "To inherit eternal life" is not the same as receiving spiritual salvation which one receives as a result of faith in Jesus Christ's death, burial, and resurrection for the forgiveness of sin. As evidenced in the account of Jesus and the rich young ruler, to inherit eternal life is the result of one's works. Inheriting eternal life speaks to the quality of one's life and not the longevity of life.

[124] Matthew 5 contains what is traditionally called "the Beatitudes," which list rewards based on the lifestyle of disciples.

[125] Johannes P. Louw and Eugene Albert Nida, *Greek-English Lexicon of the New Testament: Based on Semantic Domains* (New York: United Bible Societies, 1996), 202.

[126] William Arndt et al., A Greek-English Lexicon of the New Testament and Other Early Christian Literature (Chicago: University of Chicago Press, 2000), 851.

[127] Barclay Moon Newman and Philip C. Stine, *A Handbook on the Gospel of Matthew*, UBS Handbook Series (New York: United Bible Societies, 1992), 230.

[128] John Nolland, "The Gospel of Matthew: A Commentary on the Greek Text," *New International Greek Testament Commentary* (Grand Rapids, MI; Carlisle: W.B. Eerdmans; Paternoster Press, 2005), 357.

[129] Donald A. Hagner, Matthew 1–13, vol. 33a, *Word Biblical Commentary* (Dallas: Word, Incorporated, 1993), 205.

[130] Horst Robert Balz and Gerhard Schneider, *Exegetical Dictionary of the New Testament* (Grand Rapids, MI: Eerdmans, 1990–), 186.

[131] Barclay Moon Newman and Philip C. Stine, *A Handbook on the Gospel of Matthew*, UBS Handbook Series (New York: United Bible Societies, 1992), 231.

[132] Ibid., 256.

[133] Marty A. Cauley, *The Outer Darkness: Its Interpretations and Implications* (Sylva, NC: Misthological Press, 2012).

[134] Dillow, Joseph C. *Final Destiny: The Future Reign of The Servant Kings Revised Edition*, 790, 792. Grace Theology Press. Kindle Edition.

[135] Rodney K. Duke, "The Idiom of 'Weeping and Gnashing of Teeth' in the Gospels: A Funerary Formula," *Perspectives in Religious Studies* 47 (2020), 283.

[136] Douglas S. McCorniskey 1976. In Brown C (ed.), *The New International* Dictionary of New Testament Theology (vol. 2), 421. Grand Rapids, MI: Zondervan. [must check this reference]

[137] Zoltan L. Erdey and Kevin G. Smith, "'Weeping and Gnashing of Teeth'—the Nature of the Suffering of the Wicked in Matthew," *Conspectus 2013*, vol. 15, 156.

[138] Rodney K. Duke, "The Idiom of 'Weeping and Gnashing of Teeth," 293.

[139] To be thrown alive into the lake of fire is a form of death in that death is a separation. The separation of men from God's presence and possible forgiveness is called the second death in Revelation 20:14.

[140] Moisés Silva, "Perfection and Eschatology in Hebrews," *Westminster Theological Journal 39*, no. 1 (1976): 64.

[141] Ibid., 63.

[142] Horst Robert Balz and Gerhard Schneider, *Exegetical Dictionary of the New Testament* (Grand Rapids, MI: Eerdmans, 1990–), 51. All three Synoptic Gospels utilize the same verb, *paschō*, to describe our Lord's prediction.

[143] Horst Robert Balz and Gerhard Schneider, *Exegetical Dictionary of the New Testament* (Grand Rapids, MI: Eerdmans, 1990–), 152.

[144] Johannes P. Louw and Eugene Albert Nida, *Greek-English Lexicon of the New Testament: Based on Semantic Domains* (New York: United Bible Societies, 1996), 242.

[145] Biblical Studies Press, The NET Bible First Edition; Bible. English. NET Bible; The NET Bible (Biblical Studies Press, 2005), Ro 8:15–17.

[146] See Romans 2:7-8, 25; 5:16; 6:11; 7:25; 8:10, 17; 9:21; 11:22, 28; 14:2, 5; 16:19.

[147] George W. Knight, *The Pastoral Epistles: A Commentary on the Greek Text, New International Greek Testament Commentary* (Grand Rapids, MI; Carlisle, England: W.B. Eerdmans; Paternoster Press, 1992), 441.

[148] William D. Mounce, "Pastoral Epistles," vol. 46, *Word Biblical Commentary* (Dallas: Word, Incorporated, 2000), 560.

[149] Being a conqueror in salvation (1 John 5:4) is not the same as being a conqueror in sanctification. Salvation is a reality now; however, we must wait to see whether we will be included among those proclaimed in Revelation 3:21.

[150] Ibid, p. 432.